THE
PRESSURE COOKER
YEAST & QUICK BREAD
COOKBOOK

Achieve Fabulous Flavor-Infused Breads
in Instant Pots, Electric and Stove-Top Cookers

Em Elless

COPYRIGHT

To Ernest Jackson Smith, who always encouraged, always hoped, always persevered, always loved, no matter what. One of the kindest men in the universe.

Table of Contents

INTRODUCTION

Welcome to the delectable world of pressure-steamed bread! Although steaming bread is a popular cooking method around the world, you will soon discover, as I did, that *pressure-steamed* bread is a whole new taste reward for bread-lovers.

Many will be surprised that I have taken such a giant step away from "low-carb gluten-free" recipes, a term once thought to be an oxymoron until my first cookbook, "Muffins to Slim By." Briefly, this is how this book came about.

After I got a mini Instant Pot for Christmas and discovered all the joys and benefits, I began to explore what was out there with bread recipes, my favorite food. After some research I found that while quick bread recipes and cakes were beginning to appear online (with "Cake" buttons on new cooker models), pressure cooker yeast breads were nearly nonexistent. Apparently, they were generally considered undoable. Friends and family asked when I was going to start experimenting, but how about some "regular" breads first? Couldn't I toss in a monkey-bread recipe, or some cornbread or Hawaiian rolls? Well . . . no, not in a low carb book. But I loved the challenge. I was used to testing and deep-sixing countless pounds of alternative flours in previous books to find recipes that worked. Why not see what happened with classic bread favorites and if it could be done, tackle a quinoa/flax book later?

And so here we are. After proofing, discarding and taste-testing countless loaves morning, noon and night, every day for months, and now 30 pounds overweight, I am happy to say, with this cookbook, that we can add fabulous yeast breads to our culinary achievements. Pressure-cooked quick breads are not only scrumptious, they are impossible to find anywhere else but home.

Just as artisan and bread-machine breads are delicious but distinctly different, pressure-cooked breads are unique. They have a denser, moister texture overall, infused with flavors that cannot be achieved by any other method. Several yeast bread recipes are every bit as lofty as their oven-baked counterparts. Some rose to such heights during testing that they filled the lid and valve and every other crevice the crowded dough could squeeze into, requiring minor surgery with intricate tools to remove. Once I got the portions right, it was, and still is, an exciting moment to lift off the lid after the cooking time and find a beautiful loaf of homemade bread, far superior to most store-bought brands. I now prefer making all my bread with this method not only because it tastes better, but also because the energy savings are substantial; we're not paying for air-conditioning and a hot oven at the same time.

You may be surprised to see that the yeast bread recipes do not require a separate proofing of the yeast before adding to the dough, nor any proofing baskets or boxes. I discovered years ago that this step is not necessary if you know you are using fresh yeast, either newly purchased or stored in the freezer. The streamlined recipes are fast and easy; add all ingredients in the order given and mix away.

The primary difference you will see with this method is that the crust is not browned like oven-baked. The loaves will emerge golden or pale or rich brown, depending on the recipe. If you or loved ones usually cut off the crusts of commercial breads, you may very well change your mind. Pressure-cooked bread crusts are light and tender with a delicious chewy texture. However, there is one recipe, French Bread, that I recommend putting under a toaster-oven broiler a few minutes, if you love a crunchy crust that shatters when you bite into it as much as I do.

Please take the time to read each section (they're short and to the point!) before beginning. Understanding the process is important, and you will need the information to make choices that are right for you. So, let's begin. Pass the butter!

UNDERSTANDING THE COOKING PROCESS

No matter what type of pressure cooker you use, you have undoubtedly already prepared several wonderful meals, have studied the instruction manual, know how to adjust the heat on your gas or electric stove to bring it to High pressure and maintain it, what button to push on your electric model. Now you're ready to add homemade bread to the list of wonderful things your cooker can do. The following process is the same for every 3 qt, 5qt, 6 qt on up, is very simple but vital to your bread-making success. Steamed bread and pressure-steamed bread are two completely different methods.

•The bread pan must sit on a trivet above the water level. The temperature of water just before it boils and turns to steam is 212°. No matter how hard it boils it will never get any hotter. If the bottom of the bread pan is sitting in it, that is the temperature it's going to cook in. The dough higher up in the bread pan, surrounded by pressurized steam, can reach 250 degrees and will cook much faster. Although the bread can look and feel done on top when the lid is removed, the bottom will be damp and dense when removed from the pan. The goal is to use a trivet that will raise the bread pan high enough above the boiling water level—not just barely above it, but well above it— so that the hotter steam will circulate all around the pan.

•Use a trivet that is between 1" and 2" high, preferably made of steel, which gets very hot and transfers that heat to the bread pan.

Silicone does not work as well, and the slots are much narrower, inhibiting the free-flow of steam. You can also use mini springform pans with the bottoms removed, 9.75 oz canned chicken cans, tops and bottoms removed, or *scrunched foil. *Whichever,* the trivet must be high enough to have good steam circulation all around the pan, while allowing ample room for the bread to rise. If you are using a mini-pot, unless you have something like a pet-food can no higher than 1", top and bottom removed, your best option is to *tear off a piece of foil, scrunch it into loose ball and set it into the cooker, put the bread pan on top and lightly press down until you have a good 2" clearance between the top of the bread pan and rim of the cooker.

For the most success with pressure cooker bread making, try to use only metal or foil pans, which quickly conduct heat to the rising bread. You can also use silicone pans, but they do not conduct heat as well and take longer to "bake" the bread. Try to avoid glass or ceramic dishes as they are poor conductors of heat and will raise your cooking time a substantial amount. If you do, add more time and note when it is finished.

INGREDIENTS, PROOFING AND SET-UP

Two ingredients are listed in every yeast recipe in this book that you may not normally use or be familiar with but are very important to the finished bread. Let me briefly explain why.

BREAD FLOUR contains more gluten than all-purpose flour, a protein found in wheat which traps the bubbles of carbon dioxide that form when the yeast eats sugar (why artificial sweeteners alone won't work in yeast bread recipes). The more gluten, the higher the dough will rise, giving yeast bread the airy texture we love. All-purpose flour cannot achieve the same height and quality. There is very little, if any, difference in price between the two.

DIASTATIC MALT POWDER *(not to be confused with NON-diastatic malt, which is a sweetener)* has long been a secret of professional bakers. Although only 1 teaspoon is added in each yeast bread recipe, it adds significant flavor, texture and a savory bread aroma. It is made from sprouted grains (usually barley) that have been dried and ground. "Diastatic" refers to the active enzymes that are created as the grain sprouts, which convert starches into sugars and promote yeast growth. If it helps, think of it as important to the recipe as vanilla is to cake and cookie recipes (although it plays a much more active role). It comes in various-sized containers and is relatively inexpensive because only 1 teaspoon is used per recipe. I've made countless dozens and have hardly made a dent in a 1# bag. I store it in a tight container in my pantry. It is available on several online sites and some health food stores.

As I mentioned in the Introduction, the yeast bread recipes do not require a separate proofing process (mixing yeast with water and sugar in a separate bowl until it bubbles and "proves" it is active). Before you begin, buy fresh active dry yeast, store in a cool, dry place (I keep mine in the freezer) and use before the expiration date. Put ingredients in the order given into a large bowl and mix away.

Nor do you need separate baskets or boxes for the dough to rise. Your pressure cooker will handle this beautifully. While your mixer is kneading the dough (or before if you are kneading by hand) put a couple inches of hot tap water into the cooker to warm the pan. Discard when the dough is finished kneading, but do not dry the pan. Spritz a bowl with cooking spray, set in the dough ball, turn it to coat, set it into the cooker and place the lid on top. It will rise, gently warmed and protected from drafts.

MINI POT CHEFS: Instructions and ingredients for mini pots are in (Red Parenthesis).

NOTE FOR THOSE WITH A "YOGURT" BUTTON ON ELECTRIC MODELS: You can use this setting for the first and second rise, but check the dough a little more often, as it will double in size more quickly.

DO NOT USE THE "WARMING" BUTTON, EVER, TO RAISE DOUGH. The temperature is too hot and will kill the yeast.

●After the dough has risen the first time, shape it as directed and put into a lightly greased pan. Put 1 ½ cups water into cooker pan, set in a 1"-2" trivet, lay a foil sling *(see instructions how to make)* across middle and up sides for easy access and put bread pan *crosswise* in center. By setting this up now, when the dough has risen the second time, you won't have to disturb the bread. Just secure the lid and MAKE SURE VALVE IS ON SEAL. You will see this bold instruction on every recipe because it is easy to forget. I have started the process with my Instant Pot, gone outside with the assurance that everything was timed and doing its thing, and come back into the house to the sound of loud hissing from the kitchen. If it has been going on awhile, the bread may be ruined; there is no way of knowing other than to close the valve and wait until the cooking time is up and lifting the lid to either a lump or a loaf. Seriously. Check that valve. I'm embarrassed to admit I still sometimes forget, until I hear that sound . . .

●Every bread recipe is cooked at High pressure. The timing starts when the cooker reaches that level. If you are using a stovetop cooker, watch closely to see when High pressure is achieved and start timing at that point. Electric cookers will keep track of the time for you, and alert you when it is reached, and monitor the cooking time, too.

●When the time is up, carefully *quick-release the pressure. The reason for this is that you need to check the internal temperature of the bread to make sure it is cooked. Insert an instant-read temperature probe 2 or 3 places near the center.

If below 190°, secure the lid, CLOSE THE VALVE, and cook another few minutes. Everything is already hot, and the cooker will return quickly to High pressure. You only need to do this the first time you make the recipe. Make a note of the pan you used and the total cooking time for future reference. Another great benefit of pressure-cooked bread is that you can't "overbake" it as in regular hot ovens—one minute it's perfect, five minutes later it's dried out, ten minutes too long and it's toast. If left far too long in a pressure cooker, the texture will be tougher, but you can just slice it thinner and still enjoy it. Be sure to note a shorter cooking time.

*I DO NOT recommend carrying a stovetop cooker to the sink and setting it in cold water or pouring cold water on the lid! Hold a spoon or knife against the valve and release the pressure in short steam bursts, waiting a few seconds between each. It will take a couple minutes but is safe and relatively fast.

And before I forget, level all dry ingredients with a straight-edged knife and mind the liquids!

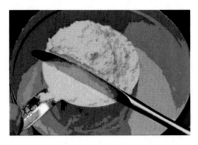

TO FOIL OR NOT TO FOIL

While researching various pressure-cooked quick bread methods online, I noted that covering the bread pans with foil before cooking—sometimes placing a paper towel first, then sealing the pan with foil—was the standard practice. Since I started my testing with yeast breads to see whether they could be done in a pressure cooker, covering them with foil was out of the question. The dough needed to rise uninhibited, hopefully high above the top of the pan. The loaves emerged from the cooker glistening with steam. Within two minutes the steam evaporated, leaving behind a tender, chewy crust with a glossy sheen. I was curious, then, to learn what would happen when I began making quick breads. I cooked the first few by my usual method and they emerged glazed with steam which again, quickly disappeared, finishing soft and dry. The only way to see the difference between the two methods was to cook two loaves at the same time, one covered with foil, the other, not.

Cornbread, Before Cooking

The uncovered loaf on the left rose higher in the middle, the covered loaf more level overall. The taste and texture were identical.

The next comparison test was with banana bread, which showed the biggest difference.

The loaf on the left was uncovered and rose high in the middle, splitting as banana bread often does. The crust was tender and glossy. The covered loaf on the right emerged with a dry top crust, more level and slightly browned here and there.

7

Comparing height, they are about the same. There was a noticeable difference in moistness and texture, however. The covered loaf on the right had a drier, denser texture, as is noticeable in the image.

There is a middle road you can take, and I list it as an "if desired" option in each recipe. Lay a piece of tin foil slightly larger than your cooker pan on top and press all around to make a circle template. Cut an inch inside the inner indent line, leaving plenty of room all around the foil circle for steam to circulate. Spray the underside of the foil with cooking spray and lay it lightly on top of the bread pan. Do not attach it in any way. The foil will rise along with the bread, won't stick because of the spray, and the loaf will come out pretty well dry on top. You can reuse the foil several times.

What it comes down to is a matter of personal preference. Experiment and find the method you like best. Most of the time I just set in the bread pan and forget it. It's not like making a cheesecake where a pristine top is important.

ABOUT PANS

One of our biggest challenges is finding bread pans that will fit inside 6 qt and smaller cookers. As of this writing there are limited options because yeast breads just aren't being done yet. Hopefully in another year or so, manufacturers will be meeting this need, but in the meantime, this is basically what we have to work with.

In addition to easy-to-find mini foil pans, mini-flute and 6" cake pans can be found in the bakery-supply section (rather than the standard pan section) of big box stores as well as online. Also check out the cooking pots in the camping department. Mini spring-form pans are another option, as well as small coffee cans, which many already use to make quick breads. See also my comments on foil pan options in the following 6 qt section.

MINI FOIL PANS   MINI FLUTE PAN

CAMPING POTS   6" CAKE PAN

What would I like to find? Loaf pans that are slightly larger than the mini size, more bundt pan choices, square pans . . .

While some standard bread pans will fit inside 8 qt and larger cookers, finding sizes for 6 qt. cookers is an interesting challenge. Since both my larger Instant Pot and stove-top cookers are 6 qt, which is the size most of us use (and because you can park a Humvee in 10+ qt cookers), I've geared my research toward pans that can slip into, or be adjusted to, an 8" diameter opening. Without thinking clearly, I bought a 7½ inch wide bread pan thinking of course it would work, which of course it didn't because, well, the square-peg-in-a-round-hole thing.

6 Cup Flute   Stack Pans

Medium Foil Loaf   Silicone Bundt

Thankfully, inexpensive medium loaf foil pans can be quickly adapted (and re-used) with minor tweaking. Unfold the top rim and bend up straight, then pinch in the corners a half inch. Test it by inserting into the pot and tweak where it hits. 1 ½ pound foil storage containers, which make wider loaves, also work (even in mini pots), adjusting the same way. Look for measurements that are close to 2" high (deep) so the bread will have side support as it rises. You will be bending up the top rim to make it higher still.

The 9" Marathon silicone bundt pan works beautifully if you don't mind a little minor surgery to fit 6 qt cookers.

Cut off the top rim with scissors

Insert into cooker pan and make an indent on each side. You will see this process in the Monkey Bread recipe images.

10

The indents are barely noticeable when the finished bread is inverted.

HOW TO MAKE A SLING/FOIL FRENCH BREAD PAN

Need: 18" Heavy-Duty Foil

Lifting straps are a must-have for removing hot pans from the cooker. The handles on trivets that come with many cookers aren't high enough. Most of the yeast breads are so lofty there is no way to take hold of the pan. Quick breads are nearly impossible to grasp even with silicone mini pinch mitts; there is a strong risk of losing the grip, splashing up hot water and, well, I'm too embarrassed to say what happened next. Just trust me on this: A LIFTING STRAP IS VITAL! Fortunately, they are fast, easy and inexpensive to make and will last through many loaves. You will know when it's time to retire them; they become quite floppy and begin to crack.

•Tear off a 12" long sheet of 18" heavy duty foil. On the long side, make a fold 2" wide and press down on the crease. Fold this over and press down the crease. Repeat four more times, then fold over the two raw ends ½" and press down.   You now have a strong sling wide enough to lift the bulkiest breads.

If you love French bread, you can make a foil pan that will fit inside a 6 qt cooker which duplicates expensive French bread loaf pans. It can be used several times by just wiping the interior.

•Tear off four 16" long pieces of 18" wide heavy-duty foil. Stack them as evenly as possible (they're not all going to be exact), then fold them over as one, short end to short end, and press down firmly on the crease. Fold again, narrow side to narrow side, and press down firmly, making another sharp crease. Fold over the raw edges ½" and press down. You now have a heavy foil rectangle approximately 7" x 8". Using a 32 oz. vinegar bottle or a 16-20 oz can, place it in the center of the foil, top and bottom facing the narrow sides of the rectangle, bring up the foil sides and press firmly to create a mold of the rounded shape.

HOW TO FREEZE BREAD DOUGH/BAKE FROZEN DOUGH

If you are a mini-pot chef, the following will be helpful if you decide to follow the full-recipe ingredients (rather than the mini-pot measurements). The directions are also the same for pressure-cooking store-bought frozen bread dough.

•For recipes in this book, follow all directions for mixing (making sure to only use active dry yeast), kneading and proceeding as directed through the first rise.

•After it has doubled in size, punch down, knead lightly and form into desired shape so you can later just defrost and cook. (Otherwise you will have to babysit and catch the dough at just the right moment of thawing, before it starts to rise. After the first couple hours this begins to feel like a hostage situation) Therefore, place the shaped dough into a lightly greased pan, cover with plastic wrap and put into freezer. When it is frozen solid, about 3-4 hours, remove loaf from pan, wrap securely with plastic wrap or foil, place into a freezer bag and date it. Properly wrapped and stored, frozen dough will be good-to-go for up to 3 months. Because bread flour has a higher gluten content, it is better able to withstand the freezing process.

•When ready to use—and this also applies to frozen store-bought loaves—put frozen dough into a lightly greased bread pan, cover with plastic wrap and thaw one of two ways: Let thaw in refrigerator for 8 to 14 hours, then finish thawing at room temperature, approximately 3 hours, until doubled in size, OR: Let covered dough rise at room temperature until doubled in size, about 6 hours. The room temperature will affect the rising time. Do not try to quick-thaw in the microwave. It won't work, it will kill the yeast. NOTE: You can also let the dough rise in the cooker, following the instructions with the recipe, but remember to set the timer. I was testing a store-bought frozen loaf and forgot about it. When I walked by a couple hours later I was startled to see a white balloon in the cooker pan. It deflated when I tried to lift it out. I did bake it by the way; the top was a little strange, but it tasted good.

•If left to rise on the counter, put 1½ cups water in cooker pan, set in 1" - 2" trivet, lay sling across middle and up sides, set bread pan in crosswise and follow cooking directions for that recipe.

EQUIVALENTS/METRICS/ALTITUDE

U.S./ STANDARD METRIC EQUIVALENTS (rounded

1/8 teaspoon = 0.5 ml

1/4 teaspoon = 1 ml

1/2 teaspoon = 2 ml

1 teaspoon = 5 ml

1 tablespoon = 1/2 fl oz = 15 ml

2 tablespoons = 1/8 cup = 1 fl oz = 30 ml

4 tablespoons = 1/4 cup = 2 fl oz = 60 ml

5 1/3 tablespoons = 1/3 cup = 3 fl oz = 80 ml

8 tablespoons = 1/2 cup = 4 fl oz = 120 ml

10 2/3 tablespoons = 2/3 cup = 5 fl oz = 160 ml

12 tablespoons = 3/4 cup = 6 fl oz = 180 ml

16 tablespoons = 1 cup = 8 fl oz = 240 ml

VOLUME & WEIGHT

	2 Tbsp	¼ cup	1/3 cup	1/2 cup	2/3 cup	¾ cup	1 cup
Butter	30g	60g	80g	120g	160g	180g	240g
Flour, All-Purpose	15g	30g	40g	60g	80g	90g	120g
Sugar Gran.	15g	50g	65g	100g	130g	150g	200g
Sugar, Brown	23g	45g	60g	90g	120g	135g	180g
Cornmeal	20g	40g	50g	80g	100g	120g	160g
Oats, Uncooked	11g	22g	30g	45g	60g	65g	90g
Fruits/Veg Chopped	20g	40g	50g	75g	100g	110g	150g
Nuts, Chopped	20 g	40 g	50 g	75 g	100 g	110 g	150 g

LENGTH CONVERSION

1 inch = 2.5 cm

2 inches = 5 cm

3 inches = 7.6 cm

4 inches = 10 cm

5 inches = 13 cm

6 inches = 15 cm

7 inches = 18 cm

8 inches = 20 cm

HIGH ALTITUDES: For every 1,000 ft above 2,000 ft, increase cooking time by 5%:

3000 ft + 5%

4000 ft + 10%

5000 ft + 15%

6000 ft + 20%

7000 ft + 25%

8000 ft + 30%

9000 ft + 35%

10,000 ft + 40%

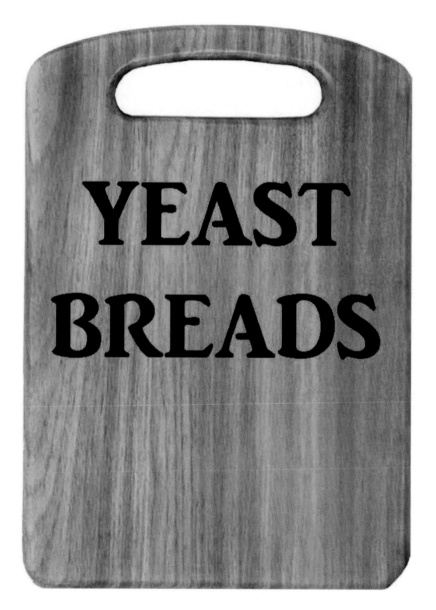

YEAST BREADS

Yeast Bread Tip: If the risen dough looks doubled in size but you're not sure, poke it with your finger about a half inch deep. If it springs right back, it needs more time to rise. If the indent remains or springs back slowly, it is fully proofed

WHITE BREAD
Nutrition Data: Sixteen ½" Slices (baked in 8" loaf pan). Made with whole milk
Each: 99 Calories; 4g Protein; 158mg Sodium; 5g Total Fat; 19gCarbs; 0g Fiber

NOTES:_____

_____

_____

_____

_____

WHITE BREAD

Absolutely delicious. Far surpasses supermarket breads in flavor and texture. Crust is puffy-tender with a light chew. Perfect for sandwiches. Rises high. Bread may stick here and there to sides of pressure pan. No matter. It will lift right out. (mini-pot measurement)

1 (½) **Cup Milk**

¼ **Cup** (2 TBS) **Water**

1 TBS (1 ½ tsp) **Butter, softened**

3 (1 ½) **Cups Bread Flour**

1 (2 tsp) **TBS Granulated Sugar**

1 (½) **tsp Diastatic Malt Powder**

1 (½) **tsp Salt**

1 *Pkt. (1 tsp) **Active Dry Yeast**

   *Pkt = 2 ¼ tsp

•Put ingredients in order given in mixer bowl. Mix and knead by hand 10 minutes *OR* mix with paddle on Low/Stir 3 minutes. May need to dislodge dough once from paddle. Switch to dough hook and knead 7 minutes on Low/Medium. If dough won't gather into a ball after a couple minutes kneading, sprinkle on 1 TBS flour and let mix in a couple minutes. This should do it but if not, sprinkle on another TBS. Most of the time the dough will knead into a smooth ball without tweaking, weather depending.

•While dough is kneading (or before if kneading by hand) put a couple inches of hot tap water into pressure cooker pan. When dough is finished kneading, discard water but do not dry pan. Put dough ball into a lightly greased bowl, turn to coat, set bowl into cooker pan and place lid on top. Let rise 1 hour or until double in size.

•Punch down dough and form into a smooth mound if using a round pan, or pat into a ½ inch thick rectangle almost as wide as bread pan. Roll narrow side into a loaf, pinch ends to seal and place, seam-side down, into the lightly greased pan. Optional: Sprinkle top with sesame or poppy seed.

•Put 1 ½ cups water in pressure cooker pan, set in riser/trivet that raises bread pan at least an inch above water level, lay sling across middle and bring up sides for easy access. Set in bread pan, put cooker lid on top and let rise 45 minutes or until double in size.

•If desired, drop a circle of foil *loosely* on top of bread pan, spray-side down. Secure lid—MAKE SURE VALVE IS ON SEAL—and cook on High pressure 30 (20) minutes. Quick-release pressure and insert probe thermometer in two or three places. If it hasn't reached 190°, secure lid, CLOSE VALVE and pressure-cook another five minutes. Lift out loaf and let rest 10 minutes on a rack, then remove bread from pan and let cool as long as possible before slicing. Record time and pan used.

TOASTED OATMEAL BUTTERMILK

Nutrition Data: Sixteen ½" Slices (baked in 8" loaf pan)
Each: 88 Calories; 3g Protein; 163mg Sodium; 1g Total Fat; 17gCarbs; 0g Fiber

NOTES:_____

_____

_____

_____

_____

_____

_____

TOASTED OATMEAL BUTTERMILK

Delicious Delectable Buoyant (measurement for mini-pots)

¾ Cup (6 TBS) Buttermilk or *Sour Milk

2 (1) TBS Water

2 (1) TBS Honey

1 TBS (1 ½ tsp) Butter, softened

¾ Cup (6 TBS) Regular Rolled Oats

2 (1) Cups Bread Flour

1 (½) tsp Diastatic Malt Powder

1 (½) tsp Salt

1 *Pkt (1 tsp) Active Dry Yeast

   *Pkt = 2 ¼ tsp

***add 1 TBS vinegar or lemon juice to ¾ cup milk and let "sour" for 5 minutes.**

• Spread rolled oats on baking sheet and bake in toaster oven 10-12 minutes, or until lightly toasted. Reserve 1 TBS and put remainder into mixing bowl.

• Put ingredients in order given in mixing bowl (adding cold milk and other ingredients on top of hot toasted oats will cool them down quickly before yeast is added). Mix and knead by hand 10 minutes *OR* mix with paddle attachment 3 minutes on Low/Stir. Dislodge dough from paddle 2-3 times. If dough still clings, sprinkle on 1 TBS flour, let it work in; this should do it. Switch to dough hook and knead 7 minutes on Low/Medium.

• While dough is kneading (or before if mixing by hand) put a couple inches of hot tap water into pressure cooker pan. Discard water when dough has finished kneading but do not dry pan. Put dough ball into a lightly greased bowl, turn to coat, set bowl into pressure cooker and place lid on top. Let rise 1 hour or until double in size.

• Remove bowl from pot and punch down dough. If using a stack pan (round), form dough into a smooth mound, set into lightly greased pan and pat down dough to within ½" from pan sides. If making a loaf, pat dough into a rectangle almost the width of the pan, ½" thick, and roll up tightly. Pinch ends to seal and place seam-side down into lightly greased pan. Sprinkle with reserved toasted oats.

• Put 1 ½ cups water in pressure cooker pot, set in a 1"—2" trivet, lay sling across center and up sides for easy access and set bread pan on top. Let rise 45 minutes or until double in size.

• If desired, drop (like a feather) a lightly greased foil disk on top of loaf. Secure lid—MAKE SURE VALVE IS ON SEAL—and cook on High pressure 35 (24) minutes. Quick release, test with probe. If temperature hasn't reached 190°, secure lid (CLOSE VALVE!) and cook another 5 minutes. Remove to rack and let cool 10 minutes before removing bread from pan to cool on rack.

EGG BREAD

Nutrition Data: Sixteen Slices (½" slice baked in 8" loaf pan) Made with whole milk.
Each: 108 Calories; 3g Protein; 129mg Sodium; 4g Total Fat; 20gCarbs;0g Fiber

NOTES:_____

_____

_____

_____

_____

_____

_____

EGG BREAD

Delicious White Bread, Perfect for Sweet Roll Recipes

(measurement for mini-pots)

¾ **Cup (6 TBS) Milk**

1 **(1) Egg, large**

¼ **Cup (1 TBS) Water**

2 **(1) TBS Butter, softened**

3 **Cups (1 ½) Bread Flour**

2 **(1) TBS Sugar**

¾ **(½) tsp. Salt**

1 **(½) tsp. Diastatic Malt Powder**

1 ***Pkt. (1 tsp) Yeast**

   Pkt = 2 ¼ tsp

•Put ingredients in order listed in mixer bowl. Mix and knead by hand 10 minutes *OR* mix with paddle on Low/Stir for 3 minutes. You may have to dislodge dough once or twice from paddle. Switch to dough hook and knead 7 minutes on Low/Medium to fully develop gluten.

•While dough is kneading (or before if kneading by hand) put a couple inches of hot tap water into cooker pan. When dough is finished kneading, discard water but do not dry pan. Put dough ball into a lightly greased bowl, turn to coat, set bowl into cooker pan and set lid on top. Let rise 1 hour or until double in size.

•Punch down dough and if making a loaf, pat dough into a rectangle almost as wide as the bread pan, ½" thick. Roll up tightly, pinch ends and bottom seam to seal and set seam-side-down into the lightly greased bread pan.

•Put 1 ½ cups water into cooker pan, set in a 1"-2" trivet, lay sling across bottom and up sides for easy access and set bread pan in center. Set lid on top and let rise 45 minutes or until double in size.

•If desired, drop a circle of foil, lightly greased on the underside, onto the pan. Do not attach in any way, just drop it in. Secure lid —MAKE SURE VALVE IS ON SEAL—and cook on High pressure 30 (20) minutes. Quick-release pressure and insert instant-read probe a couple places in center. If below 190°, secure lid, CLOSE VALVE, and cook another 5 minutes. Remove bread to cooling rack, let rest 10 minutes, then remove bread from pan to continue cooling on rack. Make a note of your total cooking time and pan used for future reference.

This is absolutely my favorite white bread, puts store-bought to shame. Expect raves!

COLONIAL BREAD

Nutrition Data: Sixteen Servings (½" slice baked in 8" loaf pan)
Each: 85.5 Calories; 3g Protein; 152mg Sodium; 1g Total Fat; 17gCarbs;1g Fiber

NOTES:_____

_____

_____

_____

_____

_____

_____

COLONIAL BREAD

Hearty yet light with complex flavors. I love this with a gravy-rich stew.

(measurement for mini-pots)

1 (½) Cup Water

1 TBS (2 tsp) Butter, softened

1 2/3 Cups (¾ Cup + 1 TBS) Bread Flour

½ (¼) Cup Whole Wheat Flour

¼ Cup (2 TBS) Rye Flour

¼ Cup (2 TBS) Cornmeal

3 TBS (1 ½ TBS) Brown Sugar

1 tsp (½) Diastatic Malt Powder

1 (½) tsp Salt

1 *Pkt. (1 tsp) Active Dry Yeast

　Pkt = 2 ¼ tsp

●Put ingredients in order given in mixer bowl. Mix and knead by hand 10 minutes *OR* mix with paddle 3 minutes on Low-Stir. Switch to dough hook and knead 7 minutes on Low/Medium.

●While dough is kneading (or before if kneading by hand) put a couple inches of hot tap water in pressure cooker pan. When dough has finished kneading, discard water but do not dry bowl. Put dough ball into a lightly-greased bowl, turn to coat and set into cooker pan. Set lid on top and let rise 1 hour, or until double in size.

●Punch down dough and pat into a ½" rectangle almost the width of your bread pan. For loaf, roll up tightly, pinch ends and bottom seal and set into loaf pan, seam-side down. Make a shallow slit down the middle with a sharp knife. For round pans, set in mound-shaped dough and pat it down evenly until edges are about half an inch from edge of pan.

●Put 1 ½ cups water in cooker pan, set in a 1-2" trivet, lay sling across middle and up sides for easy access. Set in dough pan, put lid on top and let rise 45 minutes or until double in size.

●If desired, drop in a disk of foil lightly spritzed with oil on the underside. Don't secure it in any way; just drop it in, like a feather. Secure lid—MAKE SURE VALVE IS ON SEAL— and cook on High pressure 40 (27) minutes. Quick release pressure and check internal temp with instant-read probe. If 190° or higher, lift bread out to cooling rack. If not quite there, secure lid, CLOSE VALVE, and cook another 5 minutes. Note pan you used and the total cook time.

Image 1: Before second rise.

Image 2: After rise, before cooking.

Image 3: Finished buns.

SANDWICH WHEAT BUNS
Nutrition Data: Six Buns; Made with whole milk
Each: 301 Calories; 11g Protein; 450mg Sodium; 16g Total Fat; 36gCarbs; 3g Fiber

NOTES:_____

_____

_____

_____

_____

SANDWICH WHEAT BUNS

These hearty buns will hold everything you stack on them yet are tender and buoyant. If you prefer a light, grocery-style bun, follow the white or egg bread recipe directions, let rise once, then flip back to this page for instructions making the buns. Hearty or lofty, they are so much better than most supermarket buns. You will need a set of 7.5" stack pans that fit inside 6 qt. cookers. The buns will rise slightly higher (and cook faster) in the hotter bottom pan, but taste and texture aren't affected. For mini pots, you will only be able to make one large bun which can be divided in half to serve two.
(measurement for mini pots)

1 (½) **Cup Milk**

¼ (⅛) **Cup Water**

1 (2 tsp) **TBS Honey**

2 (1) **TBS Butter, softened**

1 (½) **Cup Whole Wheat Flour**

2 (1) **Cups Bread Flour**

1 (½) **tsp Salt**

1 (½) **tsp Diastatic Malt Powder**

1 (1 tsp) ***Pkt Active Dry Yeast**

   *Pkt = 2 ¼ tsp

1 **Egg, for basting**

Sesame or Poppy Seeds

•Put all ingredients *except egg and seeds* in mixer bowl in order given. Mix and knead by hand 10 minutes *OR* mix with paddle 3 minutes on Low/Stir, then switch to dough hook and knead 7 minutes on Low/Medium.

•While dough is kneading, or before if mixing by hand, put a couple inches of hot tap water in pressure cooker to warm pan. Discard but do not dry pan when dough is done kneading.

•Put dough into a lightly greased bowl, turn to coat, set into cooker, set lid on top and let rise 1 hour. Punch down and roll into a cylinder 6 inches long. For even-sized buns, use a ruler and mark indents with a knife, 1" apart, then cut into 6 pieces. Roll each into a fairly smooth ball and pat between your hands.

•Put 3 buns into each lightly greased pan, spacing as shown in image 1. Pat down into larger bun shapes until buns almost touch. Brush tops with lightly-beaten egg and sprinkle with seeds.

•Stack the pans with flat lid on top and secure them into their rack. Put 1 ½ cups water in pressure cooker pan, set in a low trivet (no higher than ¾") and set stack-pans on top. Set pressure cooker lid on top and let buns rise 45 minutes, or until buns have doubled in size (image 2).

•Secure lid—MAKE SURE VALVE IS ON SEAL—and cook on High pressure 30 (20) minutes. Remove pans from cooker and let rest a few minutes, then remove buns from pans to a rack. Let cool before slicing

WHOLE WHEAT BREAD

Nutrition Data: Sixteen ½" Slices (baked in 8" loaf pan); Made with whole milk
Each: 104 Calories; 4g Protein; 160mg Sodium; 5g Total Fat; 19gCarbs; 2g Fiber

NOTES:_____
_____
_____
_____
_____
_____
_____

WHOLE WHEAT BREAD

Nutritious, great with everything, with a hint of molasses.
(measurement for mini pots)

1 (½) **Cup Milk**

1 TBS (½ TBS) **Molasses**

1 TBS (½ TBS) **Butter, softened**

1 ½ Cups (¾) **Whole Wheat Flour**

1 ½ Cups (¾) **Bread Flour**

1 (½) **tsp Salt**

1 (½) **tsp Diastatic Malt Powder**

1 *Pkt. (1 tsp) **Active Dry Yeast**

  *1 Pkt. = 2 ¼ tsp.

1 egg + 1 tsp water combined with fork

●Put ingredients (except egg/water) in order given in mixer bowl. Mix with paddle 3 minutes on Low/Stir. Change to dough hook and knead 7 minutes on Low/Medium.

●While dough is kneading (or before if kneading by hand) put a couple inches of hot tap water in pressure cooker pan. When dough is finished kneading, discard water but do not dry pan. Put dough ball into a lightly greased bowl, turn to coat, set bowl into cooker pan and set lid on top. Let rise 1 hour or until double in size.

●Punch down and shape dough into a mound for round pans, or pat into a rectangle almost as wide as bread pan, ½" thick. Roll up tightly, pinch ends and bottom to seal and place seam-side-down into lightly greased bread pan.

●Whip together egg and water with a fork and baste loaf with egg mixture. Sprinkle with optional seeds.

●Put 1 ½ cups water in pressure cooker pan, set in a 1-2" trivet, lay sling across center and bring up sides for easy access and put bread pan in center. Set lid on top and let rise 45 minutes or until double in size.

●If desired, drop a circle of foil, spritzed with oil on the underside, on top of pan. Secure lid—MAKE SURE VALVE IS ON SEAL—and cook on High pressure 40 (27) minutes. Quick release pressure and insert instant-read probe a couple places near center. If below 190°, secure lid, **close valve**, and cook another 5 minutes. Lift from cooker and let cool 10 minutes before removing bread from pan to cool on rack. Record time and pan used.

RYE BREAD

Nutrition Data: Ten Servings
Each: 159 Calories; 5g Protein; 251mg Sodium; 2g Total Fat; 31gCarbs;   2g Fiber

NOTES:_____

_____

_____

_____

_____

_____

_____

RYE BREAD

Fragrant to mix, wonderful with almost everything.

(measurement for mini pots)

1 (½) **Cup Water**

2 (1) **TBS Butter, softened**

2 (1) **Cups Bread Flour**

1 (½) **Cup Rye Flour**

2 (1) **TBS Brown Sugar**

2 (1) **tsp. Caraway Seeds, (or preference)**

1 (½) **tsp Diastatic Malt Powder**

1 (½) **tsp Salt**

1 *Pkt. (1 tsp) **Active Dry Yeast**

  *Pkt. = 2 ¼ tsp.

•Put ingredients in order given in mixer bowl. Mix and knead by hand 10 minutes OR mix with paddle on Low/Stir 3 minutes. You may need to dislodge dough from paddle once or twice. Switch to dough hook and knead 7 minutes on Low/Medium.

•While dough is kneading (or before if kneading by hand) put a couple inches of hot tap water into cooker pan. When dough is finished kneading, discard water but do not dry pan. Put dough ball into a lightly greased bowl, turn to coat, set bowl into cooker pan and set lid on top. Let rise 1 hour or until double in size.

•Punch down dough and if making a loaf, pat dough into a rectangle as wide as the bread pan, ½" thick. Roll up tightly, pinch ends and bottom seam to seal and set seam-side-down into the lightly greased bread pan.

•Put 1 ½ cups water into cooker pan, set in a 1"-2" trivet, lay sling across bottom and up sides for easy access and set bread pan in center. Set lid on top and let rise 45 minutes or until double in size.

•If desired, drop a circle of foil, lightly greased on the underside, onto the bread pan. Do not attach in any way, just drop it in. Secure lid —MAKE SURE VALVE IS ON SEAL—and cook on High pressure 45 (30) minutes. Quick-release pressure and insert instant-read probe a couple places in center. If below 190°, secure lid, CLOSE VALVE, and cook another 5 minutes. Remove bread to cooling rack, let rest 10 minutes, then remove bread from pan to continue cooling on rack. Make a note of your total cooking time and pan used for future reference.

ONION DILL WHEAT BREAD

Nutrition Data: Eight Generous Servings
Each: 219 Calories; 10g Protein; 388mg Sodium; 3g Total Fat; 38gCarbs; 3g Fiber

NOTES:_____

_____

_____

_____

_____

_____

_____

ONION DILL WHEAT

Buoyant, tangy-savory flavor. I bake this in a 7.5" stack pan.

(measurement for mini pots)

¾ **Cup** (6 TBS) **Cottage Cheese, small curd**

½ **Cup** (4 TBS) **Water**

1 (1) **Egg**

1 (½) **TBS Butter, softened**

1 ½ (¾) **Cups Whole Wheat Flour**

1 ½ (¾) **Cups Bread Flour**

1 (½) **TBS Brown Sugar**

1 *Pkt. (1 tsp) **Active Dry Yeast**

....*Pkt = 2¼ tsp.

1 (½) **tsp Diastatic Malt Powder**

1 (½) **tsp Salt**

1 (½) **TBS Dried Minced Onion**

2 (1) **tsp Dried Dill Weed**

●Put ingredients in order given in mixer bowl. Mix and knead by hand 10 minutes *OR* mix with paddle on Low/Stir 3 minutes. You may need to dislodge dough from paddle once or twice. Switch to dough hook and knead 7 minutes on Low/Medium.

●While dough is kneading (or before if mixing by hand) put a couple inches of hot tap water in cooker pan. Discard when dough is done kneading but do not dry pan. Put dough ball into a lightly greased bowl, turn to coat, set into cooker pan, set lid on top and let rise 1 hour or until double in size.

●Punch down dough and if making a loaf, pat dough into a rectangle as wide as the bread pan, ½" thick. Roll up tightly, pinch ends and bottom seam to seal and set seam-side-down into the lightly greased bread pan.

●Put 1 ½ cups water into cooker pan, set in a 1"-2" trivet, lay sling across bottom and up sides for easy access and set bread pan in center. Set lid on top and let rise 45 minutes or until double in size.

●If desired, drop a circle of foil, lightly greased on the underside, onto the bread pan. Do not attach in any way, just drop it in. Secure lid —MAKE SURE VALVE IS ON SEAL—and cook on High pressure 35 (24) minutes. Quick-release pressure and insert instant-read probe a couple places in center. If below 190°, secure lid, CLOSE VALVE, and cook another 5 minutes. Remove bread to cooling rack, let rest 10 minutes, then remove bread from pan to continue cooling on rack. Make a note of your total cooking time and pan used for future reference.

31

WHOLE WHEAT BUBBLE LOAF

Nutrition Data: Ten Servings; Made with whole milk
Each: 136 Calories; 5g Protein; 207mg Sodium; 8g Total Fat; 23gCarbs; 2g Fiber

NOTES:_____

_____

_____

_____

_____

_____

_____

WHOLE WHEAT BUBBLE LOAF

Fun to pull apart and dip into herbed olive oil. NOTE: To mini-pot chefs, measurements are trickier here for reducing. You may want to make the whole recipe, divide and refrigerate half for later cooking.

1 (1) Egg

1 (½) TBS Butter, softened

½ Cup + 2 TBS (¼ Cup) Milk

1 ¼ Cups (½ Cup + 2 TBS) Bread Flour

¾ Cup (6 TBS) Whole Wheat Flour

1 ½ tsp (1 tsp) Active Dry Yeast

1 (½) TBS Sugar

¾ (½) tsp Salt

1 (½) tsp Diastatic Malt Powder

For Finishing: 1 (½) TBS Melted Butter   2 (1) tsp Sesame Seed

•Put ingredients in order given (except Finishing ingredients) in mixer. Mix and knead by hand 10 minutes OR mix with paddle on Low/Stir 3 minutes. Switch to dough hook and knead on Low/Medium 7 minutes.

• While dough is kneading (or before if kneading by hand) put a couple inches of hot tap water into cooker pan. When dough is finished kneading, discard water but do not dry pan. Put dough ball into a lightly greased bowl, turn to coat, set bowl into cooker pan and set lid on top. Let rise 1 hour or until double in size.

•Punch down dough and roll by hand into an 18" (9") long rope. Cut off 1" wide pieces with scissors or pizza cutter and roll into balls. Space about half the balls in a lightly greased round pan, lightly baste rolls with half of melted butter and sprinkle tops with half of sesame seeds. Arrange remaining balls here and there on top, baste with remaining melted butter and sprinkle with remaining seeds.

•Put 1 ½ cups water in pressure cooker pan, set in 1-2" trivet, lay sling across middle and bring up sides for easy access later. Set bread pan in center, place lid on cooker and let dough rise until double in size, about 45 minutes.

•If desired, place a circle of foil, spritzed with cooking spray on the underside, on top of bread pan. Do not attach in any way, just drop it on. Secure lid—MAKE SURE VALVE IS ON SEAL—and cook on High pressure 25 (17) minutes. Quick-release pressure and test internal temp with probe. If below 190°, secure lid, CLOSE VALVE, and cook another 3 minutes. Lift bread from pot with sling and let rest 10 minutes before removing from pan to cool on a rack.

33

WHOLE WHEAT, FLAX AND OAT BREAD

Nutrition Data: Sixteen ½" Slices (baked in 8" loaf pan)
Each: 85 Calories; .5g Protein; 151mg Sodium; 1g Total Fat; 13gCarbs; 1g Fiber

NOTES:_____

_____

_____

_____

_____

_____

_____

WHOLE WHEAT, FLAX & OAT BREAD

Wholesome, nutty texture. Great with everything (measurement for mini pots)

1 (½) **Cup Water**

2 (1) **TBS Honey**

1 (½) **TBS Butter, softened**

1 ¼ **Cups** (½ **Cup + 2 TBS**) **Bread Flour**

1 (½) **Cup Whole Wheat Flour**

2 (1) **TBS Flax Meal**

2 (1) **TBS Rolled Oats**

1 (½) **tsp Diastatic Malt Powder**

1 (½) **tsp Salt**

1 *Pkt (1 tsp) **Active Dry Yeast**

...*Pkt. = 2 ¼ tsp.

●Put ingredients in order given in mixer bowl. Mix and knead by hand 10 minutes *OR* mix with paddle 3 minutes on Low/Stir. Switch to dough hook and knead 7 minutes on Low/Medium.

●While dough is kneading (or before if mixing by hand), put a couple inches of hot tap water in pressure cooker pan. Put kneaded dough ball into a lightly greased bowl and turn to coat. Discard water in cooker pan but do not dry. Set dough bowl into cooker, set lid on top and let rise 1 hour or until double in size.

●Punch down dough and pat into a rectangle ½-inch-thick, almost the width of your bread pan. Roll into a tight loaf. Pinch ends and bottom of loaf to seal and place, seam-side- down, into the lightly greased bread pan. With a sharp knife cut a shallow slit down center of the loaf. Sprinkle flax seed over top, if desired.

●Put 1 ½ cups water into cooker pan, set in a 1" to 2" trivet, lay sling across center and up sides for easy access and set in bread pan. Place lid on top and let rise 45 minutes or until double in size.

●If desired, drop a circle of foil, lightly greased on underside, on top of bread pan. Do not pat down or try to secure in any way. Just drop it like a feather. Secure lid—MAKE SURE VALVE IS ON SEAL—and cook on High pressure 35 (25) minutes. Quick release and test bread temperature with probe. If it is at or above 190°, lift out pan to cooling rack. If not quite there, secure lid, CLOSE VALVE, and cook another 5 minutes. Remove and let bread rest 10 minutes, then remove from pan to finish cooling on rack.

FRENCH BREAD

Nutrition Data: Eight 1" Slices
Each: 111 Calories; 5g Protein; 291mg Sodium; 0g Total Fat; 24gCarbs;0g Fiber

NOTES:_____
_____
_____
_____
_____
_____
_____

FRENCH BREAD

The taste and texture bread-lovers dream about when only French bread will do. This is the only recipe in this book that I recommend putting under a broiler for 8-10 minutes to give the crust a delectable crunch. *See easy instructions for making French loaf pans.* (mini pot measurement)

¾ Cup (6 TBS) Warm Water

2 (1) Cups Bread Flour

1 (½) tsp Salt

1 (½) tsp Diastatic Malt Powder

1 (1) tsp Active Dry Yeast

Cornmeal, Egg White and Optional Seeds

•Put first 5 ingredients in order given in mixer bowl. Mix and knead by hand 10 minutes *OR* mix with paddle 3 minutes on Low/Stir, then change to dough hook and knead 7 minutes on Low/Medium.

•While dough is kneading (or before if kneading by hand) put a couple inches of hot tap water in pressure cooker pan. Discard when dough is finished kneading but do not dry.

•Put dough ball in lightly greased bowl, turn to coat, set into pressure cooker, place lid on top and let rise 1 hour, or until more than double in size. Punch down and form into a smooth loaf shape a couple inches shorter than your lightly-greased bread pan. Sprinkle corn meal on bottom of pan and set loaf in pan. Put 1 ½ cups water into pressure cooker pan, set in a 1"-2" trivet. Lay sling across center and up sides for easy access later. Set in bread pan, place lid on top and let rise 60 minutes or until more than double in size.

•With a very sharp knife or razor, cut 3 shallow slashes diagonally across loaf, an inch or so apart. If desired, drop a circle of foil spritzed with cooking spray on the underside on top of bread pan. Do not attach in any way. Secure lid —MAKE SURE VALVE IS ON SEAL—and cook on high pressure 30 (20) minutes. Quick-release pressure and test center with temperature probe. If not above 190°, secure lid again (CHECK VALVE) and cook another 3 minutes.

•When loaf if finished, lift pan out to counter and baste top and sides with lightly beaten egg white. Sprinkle with seeds and set bread pan beneath a toaster-oven broiler for 10 minutes, turning occasionally for even browning. Remove and let cool before slicing. Some recommend waiting two hours. I think that's asking too much.

SWEET POTATO ROLLS

Nutrition Data: Ten Servings
Each: 180 Calories; 6g Protein; 265mg Sodium; 3g Total Fat; 24gCarbs; 2g Fiber

NOTES:_____

_____

_____

_____

_____

_____

_____

SWEET POTATO ROLLS

**Buoyant, beautiful, rich in flavor
For my 6 qt cooker I use a scalloped-edge 8" round foil pan with the flared edges easily bent upwards to fit inside the cooker. Use 6" round pan for mini-pots.** (mini pot measurement)

1 (½) **Cup Sweet Potato, mashed**

   (1 medium (small) sweet potato)

⅓ **Cup** (1 TBS) **Cooking Liquid**

1 (1) **Egg, large**

2 (1) **TBS Butter, softened**

2 (1) **TBS Brown Sugar**

2 (1) **Cups Bread Flour**

1 (½) **Cup Whole Wheat Flour**

1 (½) **tsp Diastatic Malt Powder**

1 (½) **tsp Salt**

1 *Pkt. (1 tsp) **Active Dry Yeast**

   *Pkt. = 2 ¼ tsp

●Cut sweet potato into chunks and boil in about 2 cups water until tender. Reserve liquid. Mash potato; reserve any extra for a healthful snack.

●Let mashed potatoes cool slightly, then put into mixing bowl with measurement of cooking liquid. Add remaining ingredients in order given. Mix and knead by hand 10 minutes OR mix with paddle 3 minutes on Low/Stir. If mixture is too dry, add 1 tsp of cooking liquid at a time until dough forms a clump that gathers into a ball. If too sticky (still clings to paddle after 3 minutes without forming ball), add 1 TBS bread flour until dough gathers and begins to knead.

Change to dough hook and knead 7 minutes on Low/Medium.

●While dough is kneading, or before if mixing by hand, put a couple inches of hot tap water into cooker pan. When dough is finished kneading, discard water but do not dry pan. Put dough ball into a lightly greased bowl, turn to coat, set inside cooker, place lid on top and let rise 1 hour or until double in size.

●Lightly flour surface and roll dough into a log 12 (6) inches long. Cut into 1" pieces with scissors or a pizza cutter. Roll each into a ball and set into lightly greased pan, fitting them close together.

●Put 1 ½ cups water in cooker pan, set in a 1" to 2" trivet, lay sling across center and up sides for easy access and set in bread pan. Place lid on top and let rise 45 minutes or until doubled in size. If desired, place a circle of foil (do not attach) spritzed with cooking spray on the underside on top of bread pan. Secure lid —MAKE SURE PRESSURE VALVE IS ON SEAL—and cook on High pressure 30 (20) minutes. Quick-release pressure and insert instant-read temperature probe two or three places near center. If below 190°, secure lid, CLOSE VALVE, and cook another 5 minutes. Lift out to cooling rack and let rest 10 minutes before removing bread from pan to finish cooling on rack. For a delicious spread, combine equal amounts of brown sugar and butter.

PUMPERNICKEL BREAD

Nutrition Data: Ten Generous Servings
Each: 166 Calories; 5g Protein; 241mg Sodium; 1g Total Fat; 35gCarbs; 2g Fiber

NOTES:_____

_____

_____

_____

_____

_____

_____

PUMPERNICKEL BREAD

Rich in flavor, incredible with hearty meals and piled-high hot sandwiches. I usually make this in a round stack pan and emboss the center with a stamp, as pictured. (measure for mini pots)

¾ **Cup** (6 TBS) **Water**

1 (½) **TBS Cooking Oil**

¼ **Cup** (2 TBS) **Molasses**

2 (1) **Cups Bread Flour**

1 (½) **Cup Rye Flour**

2 (1) **tsp Caraway Seeds**

1 (½) **tsp Cocoa**

1 (½) **tsp Diastatic Malt Powder**

1 (½) **tsp Salt**

1 *Pkt (1 tsp) **Active Dry Yeast**

   *Pkt. = 2 ¼ tsp

●Put ingredients in order given in mixer bowl. Mix and knead by hand 10 minutes OR mix 3 minutes on Stir/Low with paddle, then switch to dough hook and knead 7 minutes on Low/Medium.

●While dough is kneading (or before if mixing by hand) put a couple inches of hot tap water into cooker pan. When dough is finished kneading, discard water but do not dry pan. Put dough into lightly greased bowl, turn to coat, set bowl into cooker pan and place lid on top. Let rise 1 hour or until double in size.

●Punch down risen dough and conform shape to lightly greased baking pan. Emboss with stamp or cut 3 horizontal slashes on top. Put 1 ½ cups water in pressure cooker pan, set in a 1" to 2" trivet, place sling across center and up sides for easy access, and set bread pan in place. Place lid on top and let rise 45 minutes or until double in size.

●If desired, drop a circle of foil spritzed with cooking spray on the underside on top of bread pan. Do not attach to pan. Secure lid—MAKE SURE VALVE IS ON SEAL—and cook on High pressure 40 (27) minutes. Quick release and insert quick-read temperature probe two or three places near center. If below 190° secure lid, CLOSE VALVE and cook another 5 minutes.

●Lift bread from cooker and let cool 10 minutes before removing bread from pan to cooling rack.

41

POTATO BREAD

Nutrition Data: Sixteen ½" Slices (baked in 8" loaf pan); Made with whole milk.
Each: 113 Calories; 4g Protein; 168mg Sodium; 4g Total Fat; 20gCarbs; 0g Fiber

NOTES:_____

_____

_____

_____

_____

_____

_____

POTATO BREAD

Delicious white bread, perfect for sandwiches. Makes a beautiful high loaf.

(mini pot measurement)

2/3 (1/3) Cup Milk

1/2 Cup (3 TBS) Water

1 (1) Egg, large

2 (1) TBS Butter, softened

3 Cups (1 ½) Bread Flour

1/2 (¼) Cup Instant Mashed Potato Flakes

1 (½) TBS Granulated Sugar

1 (½) tsp Salt

1 (½) tsp Diastatic Malt Powder

1 *Pkt (1 tsp) Active Dry Yeast

   *Pkt. = 2 1/4 tsp

•Put ingredients in order given in mixer bowl. Mix and knead by hand 10 minutes OR mix 3 minutes with paddle on Low/Stir. May need to dislodge dough from paddle once or twice. Switch to dough hook and knead 7 minutes on Low/Medium. If dough is sticky after kneading a couple minutes, add 1 TBS of flour.

•While dough is kneading, put a couple inches of hot tap water in pressure cooker pan to warm pan slightly. Discard when dough is done kneading but do not dry pan. Put dough ball into a greased bowl, turn to lightly coat, set into pressure cooker, place lid on top and let rise 60 minutes or until double in size.

•On lightly floured surface, pat down dough into a rectangle 1/2-inch-thick, almost the width of bread pan. Roll tightly into a loaf, pinch ends and bottom seam to seal and set into lightly greased pan, seam-side down.

• Put 1 ½ cups water in cooker pan, set in a 1" trivet (the dough will rise into a high loaf so use a lower trivet, high enough to hold bread pan above boiling water level), lay sling across middle and up sides for easy access, then set bread pan in center. If desired, lightly drop a circle of foil, spritzed with cooking spray on the underside, over top of bread pan. Place lid on top and let rise 30-45 minutes or until double in size.

•Secure lid—MAKE SURE PRESSURE VALVE IS ON SEAL—and cook on High pressure 40 (27) minutes. Quick release and insert temperature probe two or three places near center. If below 190°, secure lid, CLOSE VALVE, and cook another 5 minutes. If a little browning is desired, set loaf beneath broiler of a toaster oven for 7-8 minutes, but bread is delicious browned or not. Brush top with butter, let rest 10 minutes and remove bread from pan onto rack to cool.

43

POTATO, SOUR CREAM & CHIVES ROLLS

Nutrition Data: Ten Servings; Made with whole milk
Each: 170 Calories; 7g Protein; 258mg Sodium; 6g Total Fat; 32gCarbs; 0g Fiber

NOTES:_____

_____

_____

_____

_____

_____

_____

POTATO, SOUR CREAM & CHIVES ROLLS

Lofty, Soft, Delectable Use Stack Pan or tweaked foil cake pan. Mini pots use 6" round pan. (measurement for mini pot)

2/3 (1/3) Cup Milk

1/3 Cup (3 TBS) Sour Cream

1/3 Cup (2 TBS) Water

1 (1) Egg, large

3 (1½) Cups Bread Flour

1/2 (¼) Cup Instant Potato Flakes

1 (½) TBS Granulated Sugar

1 (½) tsp Salt

1 (½) tsp Diastatic Malt Powder

2 (1) TBS Chives, dried or fresh

1 *Pkt (1 tsp) Active Dry Yeast

  ***Pkt. = 2 ¼ tsp**

●Put ingredients in order given in mixer bowl. Mix and knead by hand 10 minutes OR mix with paddle on Low/Stir 3 minutes. Dislodge dough clinging to paddle once or twice. Switch to dough hook and knead 7 minutes on Low/Medium.

●While dough is kneading, put a couple inches of hot tap water in pressure cooker pan. When dough is finished kneading, discard water but do not dry pan. Put dough ball into lightly greased bowl, turn to coat, set into cooker pan and place lid on top. Let rise 60 minutes or until double in size.

●Lightly grease chosen bread pan. Punch down dough and pull off small portions, roll into balls somewhat smaller than golf balls and evenly space around pan. Put 1 ½ cups water in pressure cooker pan, set in a short 1" high trivet (dough rises substantially), lay sling across middle and up sides for easy access later, put bread pan in place, place lid on top and let rise 30-45 minutes or until double in size.

●If desired, lightly lay a circle of foil spritzed with cooking spray on the underside on top of bread pan. Do not attach in any way. Secure lid—MAKE SURE VALVE IS ON SEAL—and cook on High pressure 30 (20) minutes. Quick-release and insert temperature probe a couple places near center. If below 190°, secure lid, CLOSE VALVE and cook another 5 minutes. Lift bread out to cooling rack, let rest 10 minutes, then remove bread from pan and baste top with butter. Expect raves. Delicious rolls!

PEANUT BUTTER & HONEY BREAD

Nutrition Data: Sixteen ½" Slices (baked in 8" loaf pan; Made with whole milk.
Each: 172 Calories; 7g Protein; 187mg Sodium; 6g Total Fat; 23.5gCarbs; 1g Fiber

NOTES:_____

_____

_____

_____

_____

_____

_____

PEANUT BUTTER AND HONEY BREAD

A crunchy delicious snack bread, great toasted with butter and jam.
(measurement for mini pots)

1 (1/3) Cup Milk

1 (1) Egg, large

1/3 Cup (3 TBS) Peanut Butter

2 (1) TBS Honey

3 Cups + 3 TBS (1½ Cups + 2 TBS) Bread Flour

1 (½) tsp Diastatic Malt Powder

1 (½) tsp Salt

**1 *Pkt (1 tsp) Active Dry Yeast
*Pkt. = 2 ¼ tsp**

3/4 Cup (6 TBS) Chopped Peanuts

•Put ingredients in order given in mixer bowl. Mix and knead by hand 10 minutes OR mix with paddle 3 minutes on Low/Stir (may need to dislodge dough once or twice). Switch to dough hook and knead 7 minutes on Low/Medium.

•While dough is kneading, or before if mixing by hand, put a couple inches of hot tap water in pressure cooker pan. When dough is done kneading, discard water but do not dry pan.

•Put dough in lightly greased bowl, set into cooker pan, place lid on top and let rise 1 hour or until double in size.

•Punch down and on lightly floured surface pat into a rectangle ½" thick, almost the width of your bread pan. Roll tightly into a loaf, pinch ends and bottom seam to seal and place, seam-side-down, into lightly greased pan.

•Put 1½ cups water in cooker pan, set in a 1" to 2" trivet, lay sling across center and bring up sides for easy access, set in bread pan, place lid on top and let rise 45 minutes or until double in size.

•If desired, drop a circle of foil, spritzed with cooking spray on the underside, lightly on top of bread pan. Do not attach to pan; just drop it on top. Secure lid—MAKE SURE VALVE IS ON SEAL—and cook on High pressure 45 (30) minutes. Quick release and insert instant-read thermometer one or two places near center. If below 190°, secure lid, CLOSE VALVE, and cook another five minutes. Lift out to cooling rack and let rest 10 minutes before removing from pan to cool.

PUMPKIN-PECAN BREAD

Nutrition Data: Eight Generous Servings; Made with whole milk.
Each: 287 Calories; 9g Protein; 331mg Sodium; 15g Total Fat; 38gCarbs; 2g Fiber

NOTES:_____

_____

_____

_____

_____

_____

PUMPKIN-PECAN BREAD

I especially love this with Brown Sugar- Butter (equal amounts of each, combined) when I have a sweet tooth. *(mini pot measurement)*

1/2 (¼) Cup Milk

1/2 (¼) Cup Canned Pumpkin

1 (1) Egg, large

2 (1) TBS Butter

3 (1½) Cups Bread Flour

1 (½) tsp Salt

1 (½) tsp Diastatic Malt Powder

1 (½) tsp Cinnamon

1/2 (¼) tsp Nutmeg

1/2 (¼) tsp Ginger

¼ (⅛) tsp Ground Cloves

1 *Pkt (1 tsp) Active Dry Yeast *Pkt. = 2 ¼ tsp

¾ (1/3) Cup Chopped Pecans

●Put ingredients in order given in mixer bowl. Mix and knead by hand 10 minutes OR mix with paddle 3 minutes on Low/Stir. Switch to dough hook and knead on Low/Medium for 7 minutes.

●While dough is kneading (or before if kneading by hand), put a couple inches of hot tap water in pressure cooker pan. Discard when dough is done kneading but do not dry bowl.

●Put dough ball into lightly greased bowl, turn to coat, set into cooker pan, place lid on top and let rise 60 minutes or until double in size.

●Punch down, form into a mound and put into a lightly greased stack pan or foil cake pan. If desired, score top with curved lines to mimic a pumpkin.

●Put 1 ½ cups water into cooker pan, set in a 1" trivet, lay sling across bottom and up sides for easy access and set in bread pan. Place lid on top and let rise 45 minutes or until double in size.

●If desired, lay a circle of foil spritzed with cooking spray on the underside on top of bread pan. Do no attach, just lay it on top. Secure lid —MAKE SURE VALVE IS ON SEAL—and cook on High pressure 45 (30) minutes. Quick release and insert instant-read thermometer a couple places near center. If below 190°, secure lid, CLOSE VALVE, and cook another 5 minutes. Lift out to rack, let rest 10 minutes, then remove bread from pan to cool on rack.

HAWAIIAN BREAD

Nutrition Data: Eight Generous Servings
Each: 260 Calories; 9g Protein; 334mg Sodium; 7g Total Fat; 42gCarbs; 0g Fiber

NOTES:_____

_____

_____

_____

_____

_____

_____

HAWAIIAN BREAD

A taste-escape to the tropics with hints of pineapple and coconuts in a moist, sweet bread. For rolls use a stack pan or tweaked round foil pan (6" round pan for mini-pots. Note to Mini Pot Chefs: I recommend preparing-the entire recipe, and after the first rise, dividing and freezing half the dough for later baking. ***See the "Freezing Dough" section of the book for instructions)***

1/2 Cup Pineapple Juice

1/2 Cup Coconut Milk

2 TBS Butter, softened

2 Large Eggs, one separated

3 Cups Bread Flour

1/4 Cup Sugar, + 1 tsp set aside

3 TBS Instant Potato Flakes

1 tsp Salt

1 *Pkt Active Dry Yeast

 *Pkt. = 2 ¼ tsp

•Microwave pineapple juice 2 minutes to kill enzymes that destroy gluten. Allow to cool while gathering ingredients.

•Separate 1 egg and set aside the yolk in a small dish. Add egg white, the other egg, cooled pineapple juice and all other ingredients in order given in mixer bowl. Mix and knead by hand 10 minutes OR mix with paddle 3 minutes on Low/Stir. Change to dough hook and knead 7 minutes on Low/Medium.

•While dough is kneading, or before if mixing by hand, put a couple inches of hot tap water in pressure cooker pan to warm it. Discard water when kneading is finished but don't dry pan.

•Put slightly sticky dough in lightly greased bowl, turning to coat. Set bowl inside cooker pan, place lid on top and let rise 1 ½ hours or until double in size. NOTE: Sweet doughs are slow risers but well worth the extra wait time.

•Punch down. (Mini pot chefs, divide and follow freezing instructions. On a lightly floured surface roll dough into a log shape 12" (6" for mini pots) long. Cut into equal 1" pieces with scissors or a pizza cutter. Roll into smooth balls and arrange in a lightly greased stack-pan or foil cake pan.

•Put 1 ½ cups water in pressure cooker pan, set in a 1" to 2" trivet, arrange sling across bottom and up sides for easy access, set bread pan in middle. Place lid on cooker and let rise 1+ hours or until double in size.

•Lightly whip egg yolk with 1 tsp sugar until well mixed. Baste tops of each roll. If desired, lay a circle of foil, spritzed with cooking spray on the underside, on top of bread pan. Do not attach in any way; just lay it on top.

•Secure lid—MAKE SURE VALVE IS ON SEAL—and cook on High pressure 35 (24) minutes. Quick release and insert instant-read thermometer a couple places near center. If it hasn't reached 190°, secure lid, CLOSE VALVE and cook another 5 minutes. Lift from cooker, let rest 10 minutes, then remove bread from pan to cool on a rack.

MEXICAN CORNBREAD

Nutrition Data: Ten Servings; Made with whole milk.
Each: 229 Calories; 7g Protein; 368mg Sodium; 9g Total Fat; 37gCarbs; 1g Fiber

NOTES:_____

_____

_____

_____

_____

_____

_____

MEXICAN CORNBREAD

Seriously delicious, rich with cheese, golden corn and a hint of crushed red pepper (mini pot measurement)

2/3 (1/3) Cup Milk

1 (½) Cup Shredded Mexican Blend Cheese

¼ Cup (2 TBS) Water

3/4 Cup (6 TBS) Whole-Kernel Corn

1 (1) Egg

2 ¼ Cups + 2 TBS Bread Flour

   (1 Cup + 3 TBS)

3/4 Cup (6 TBS) Corn Meal

3 TBS (1 ½ TBS) Granulated Sugar

1 (½) tsp Salt

1/2 tsp (¼) Crushed Red Pepper

1 *Pkt (1 tsp) Active Dry Yeast

   *Pkt. = 2 ¼ tsp

●Drain corn in a strainer, pressing down to remove excess liquid. Set aside 1 TBS, plus 1 TBS of shredded cheese, to sprinkle on bread before cooking.

●Put ingredients in order given in mixing bowl. Mix and knead by hand 10 minutes *OR*

mix with paddle attachment 3 minutes on Low/Stir, then switch to dough hook and knead 7 minutes on Low/Medium. Dough will be slightly sticky.

●While dough is kneading (or before if kneading by hand), put a couple inches of hot tap water in pressure cooker pan. Discard when dough is done kneading. Do not dry pan. Put dough into a lightly greased bowl, turn to coat, set into pressure cooker, place lid on top and let rise 1 hour or until double in size.

●Punch down dough, shape into a mound and put into a lightly-greased round pan, patting dough to within half an inch of edge. Sprinkle top with reserved corn and cheese.

●Put 1 ½ cups water in pressure cooker pan, set in a 1" trivet, lay sling across bottom and up sides for easy access and set bread pan in center. Place lid on top and let rise 1 hour or until double in size.

●If desired, lay a circle of foil, spritzed with cooking spray on the underside, on top of bread pan. Do not attach. Secure lid—MAKE SURE VALVE IS ON SEAL—and cook on High pressure 60 (40) minutes. Quick-release pressure and insert an instant-read probe a couple places near center. If below 190°, secure lid, CLOSE VALVE, and cook another 5 minutes. Remove to rack, let cool 10 minutes, then remove bread from pan to rack. Serve warm.

CHEESE BREAD

Nutrition Data: Sixteen ½" slices (baked in 8" loaf pan) Made with whole milk.
Each: 137 Calories; 7g Protein; 222mg Sodium; 7g Total Fat; 19gCarbs;0g Fiber

NOTES:_____

_____

_____

_____

_____

_____

_____

CHEESE BREAD

Light, chewy, great for sandwiches. Use your favorite cheese. Great toast! (mini pot measurement)

2/3 (1/3) Cup Milk

1 ½ (¾) Cups Shredded Cheese

¼ (⅛) Cup Water

1 (1) Egg

3 (1 ½) Cups Bread Flour

2 (1) TBS Sugar

1 (½) tsp Diastatic Malt Powder

1 (½) tsp Salt

1 *Pkt (1 tsp) Active Dry Yeast

    *Pkt. = 2¼ tsp

•Put ingredients in order given in mixer bowl. Mix and knead by hand 10 minutes OR mix with paddle 3 minutes on Low/Stir, then switch to dough hook and knead on Low/Medium 7 minutes.

•While dough is kneading (or before if kneading by hand), put a couple inches of hot tap water in pressure cooker pan. When dough is finished kneading, discard water but do not dry pan.

•Put dough ball into a lightly greased bowl, turn to coat, set bowl into pressure cooker pan, place lid on top and let rise 1 hour or until double in size.

•Punch down dough, form into a mound shape and place into a lightly greased round pan, pressing dough almost to edge of pan. Put 1 ½ cups water in pressure cooker pan, set in a 1" high trivet, place sling across bottom and up sides for easy access and put bread pan in center. Place lid on top and let rise 45 minutes or until double in size.

•If desired, lay a circle on foil, spritzed with cooking spray on the underside, on top of bread pan. Do not attach. Secure lid—MAKE SURE VALVE IS ON SEAL—and cook on High pressure 50 (34) minutes. Quick-release pressure and insert a quick-read temperature probe a couple places near center. If below 190°, secure lid, CLOSE VALVE, and cook another 5 minutes. Lift pan out to rack, let rest 10 minutes, then remove bread from pan to cool on rack.

PESTO BREAD

Nutrition Data: Ten Slices
Each: 203 Calories; 5g Protein; 269mg Sodium; 7g Total Fat; 29gCarbs; 2g Fiber

NOTES:_____

_____

_____

_____

_____

_____

_____

PESTO BREAD

Melt-in-your-mouth savory. This and a crisp salad make a delicious meal. (mini pot measure)

1 (½) **Cup Water**

2 (1) **TBS Olive Oil**

1 (½) **TBS Honey**

2 (1) **Cups Bread Flour**

1 (½) **Cup Whole Wheat Flour**

1 (½) **tsp Diastatic Malt Powder**

1 (½) **tsp Salt**

1 (½) **TBS Fresh Chopped Basil Leaves**

   or 1 (½) tsp Dried Basil

1 *Pkt (1 tsp) **Active Dry Yeast**

   *Pkt. = 2 ¼ tsp

•Put ingredients in order given in mixer bowl. Mix and knead by hand 10 minutes OR mix 3 minutes with paddle on Low/Stir. Change to dough hook and knead 7 minutes on Low/Medium. While dough is kneading, put a couple inches of hot tap water in pressure cooker pan. Discard when dough is finished kneading but do not dry pan.

•Put dough ball into a lightly greased bowl, turn to coat, set into cooker, place lid on top and let rise 45-60 minutes or until double in size. While dough is rising, prepare the pesto spread. Lightly spritz bread pan with oil.

•Punch down dough and pat into a ½" thick rectangle almost as wide as your bread pan. Spread pesto to within ½" of edges. Roll into a loaf, pinch ends and bottom seam to seal and place in pan, seam side down. Make 2 shallow diagonal slashes on top of loaf.

•Put 1 ½ cups water into pressure cooker pan, set in a 1" high trivet, lay sling across middle and up sides for easy access, set bread pan in place, put lid on top and let rise 45 minutes or until double in size.

•If desired, lay a circle on foil, spritzed with cooking spray on the underside, on top of bread pan. Do not attach. Secure lid—MAKE SURE VALVE IS ON SEAL—and cook on High pressure 50 (34) minutes. Quick-release pressure and insert an instant-read temperature probe a couple places near center. If below 190°, secure lid, CLOSE VALVE, and cook another 5 minutes. Lift pan out to rack, let rest 10 minutes, then remove bread from pan to cool on rack.

PESTO SPREAD

¼ Cup (2 TBS) **Butter, softened**

2 (1) **TBS Fresh Chopped Basil or 2 (1) tsp Dried Basil**

1 (½) **TBS Parsley Flakes**

1 (½) **TBS Fresh Chopped Chives**

...or 1 (½) **tsp Dried Chives**

1 (½) **tsp Garlic Powder**

•Blend well with fork.

MONKEY BREAD WITH BROWN SUGAR GLAZE

Nutrition Data: Ten Servings; Made with whole milk and Half & Half for glaze.
Each: 283 Calories; 7g Protein; 239mg Sodium; 5g Total Fat; 44gCarbs; 0g Fiber

NOTES:_____

_____

_____

_____

_____

_____

_____

MONKEY BREAD WITH BROWN SUGAR GLAZE

Everyone's favorite decadent treat. A little more prep time, a lot of reward. I use a silicone bundt pan *(see Pans section)*, much roomier than a 6-cup bundt pan, which also works but it will be brimming! (mini pot measurement)

1 (½) Recipe Egg Bread

½ (¼) Cup Sugar

2 (1) tsp. Cinnamon

•Mix Egg Bread recipe and follow instructions for first rise. When double in size, punch down and divide in half (mini pot chefs do not need to divide dough.)

•Combine cinnamon and sugar in a 1-gallon storage bag, shake to mix and set aside.

•Butter the baking pan/silicone pan. Put a 1" trivet (no higher) into cooker pan, add 1 ½ cups water, lay sling across center and up sides until ends are almost to top rim of the cooker pan. Set in the buttered pan and pull up ends of sling so they will be reachable after final cooking. By setting everything up now, the process will be much easier, especially lifting out the cooked bread.

•Roll dough portion/s back and forth to create 2 ropes (1 rope), each about 1 ½ feet long, an inch or so in diameter. Cut dough rope with scissors or pizza cutter into ½ inch wide pieces. Roll each into a ball. They will be about the size of walnut. Drop a few into the bag of sugar/cinnamon, shake to coat each ball, then place in buttered pan. Repeat until all dough balls are coated and evenly distributed in baking pan.

•Set cover on cooker and let rise until double in size, about 40 minutes.

•Secure lid—MAKE SURE VALVE IS ON SEAL— and cook on High pressure 30 (20) minutes. Quick-release pressure and insert temperature probe two or three places. If below 190°, secure lid, CLOSE VALVE, and cook another 5 minutes. Grab ends of sling and lift bread to rack. Let rest a few minutes, then invert onto a large plate. Drizzle with Brown Sugar Glaze.

BROWN SUGAR GLAZE

3 (1 ½) TBS Butter
2 (1) TBS Brown Sugar
¼ Cup (2 TBS) Evaporated Milk/Cream/Half & Half
½ (¼) tsp Vanilla (add to milk)
Remainder of Cinnamon/Sugar in bag
•Combine sugars & butter in small pan on low heat until butter melts and mixture begins to bubble. Slowly stir in vanilla milk, stirring constantly as mixture comes to slow boil. Continue stirring on low heat 5 minutes, remove from heat and set aside. A nice time to do this is while bread is baking. It will be a nice warm glaze at the perfect time to eat it!

OATMEAL BANANA NUT BREAD

Nutrition Data: Ten Servings; Made with pecans.
Each: 230 Calories; 8g Protein; 275mg Sodium; 6g Total Fat; 37gCarbs; 3g Fiber

NOTES:_____

_____

_____

_____

_____

_____

_____

OATMEAL BANANA NUT

Absolutely delicious, wholesome bread (mini pot measurement)

2/3 (¼) Cup Buttermilk or *Sour Milk

½ (¼) Cup Mashed Ripe Banana (1 medium (small) size)

1 (1) Egg, large

2 (1) TBS Butter, softened

1 (½) TBS Honey

1/3 Cup (3 TBS) Oatmeal, quick-cooking or regular

2 (1) Cups Bread Flour

1 (½) Cup Whole Wheat Flour

1 (½) tsp Salt

1 (½) tsp Diastatic Malt Powder

1 (½) tsp Cinnamon

¼ (⅛) tsp Nutmeg

1 *Pkt (1 tsp) Active Dry Yeast

   ***Pkt. = 2 ¼ tsp**

1/3 Cup (3 TBS) Chopped Pecans or Walnuts

   ***Sour Milk: Put 1 TBS white vinegar or lemon juice in a 2/3 Cup measure. Fill cup with milk and let thicken for 5 minutes) (Put 1 tsp lemon juice or vinegar in a ¼ measure, fill with milk and let thicken 5 minutes.)**

•Put ingredients in order given in mixer bowl. Mix and knead by hand 10 minutes OR mix 3 minutes on Low/Stir with paddle. Dislodge dough if needed. Switch to dough hook and knead 7 minutes on Low/Medium.

•While dough is kneading, or before if kneading by hand, put a couple inches of hot tap water in pressure cooker pan. Discard water when dough is finished kneading, but don't dry pan. Put dough ball into a lightly greased bowl, turn to coat, set bowl into cooker, place lid on top and let rise 1 hour or until double in size.

•Punch down dough and pat or roll into rectangle ½ inch thick, almost the width of your bread pan. Roll snugly into a loaf, pinch ends and bottom seam to seal and set, seam-side-down, into lightly greased pan.

•Put 1½ cups water into pressure cooker pan, put in a 1" to 2" trivet, lay sling across center and up sides for easy access and set bread pan in middle. Place lid on top and let rise 45 - 60 minutes or until double in size.

•If desired, lay a circle of foil spritzed with cooking spray on the underside, on top of bread pan. Do not attach. Secure lid —MAKE SURE VALVE IS ON SEAL— and cook on High pressure 55 (37) minutes. Quick-release pressure and insert quick-read probe a couple places near center of loaf. If under 190°, secure lid, CLOSE VALVE and cook another five minutes. Lift pan out to rack, let rest 10 minutes, then remove bread from pan to finish cooling on rack.

CINNAMON SWIRL LOAF

Nutrition Data: Sixteen ½" Servings (baked in 8" loaf pan); With whole milk & pecans.

Each: 280 Calories; 3g Protein; 563mg Sodium; 12g Total Fat; 41gCarbs;1g Fiber

NOTES:_____

_____

_____

_____

_____

_____

CINNAMON SWIRL LOAF

Pure comfort food. Crunchy perfection when toasted. (mini pot measurement)

BREAD:

¾ **Cup (5 TBS) Milk**

¼ **(1/8) Cup Water**

2 **(1) TBS Butter, softened**

1 **(1) Egg, large**

3 **(1 ½) Cups Bread Flour**

2 **(1) TBS Sugar**

1 **(½) tsp Diastatic Malt Powder**

1 **(½) tsp Salt**

1 ***Pkt (1 tsp) Active Dry Yeast**

   *Pkt. = 2¼ tsp.

Filling:

1/3 **Cup (3 TBS) Walnuts or Pecans, chopped**

1/3 **Cup (3 TBS) Brown Sugar**

2 **(1) tsp Cinnamon**

2 **(1) TBS Butter, softened**

•Put bread ingredients in order given into mixing bowl. Mix and knead by hand 10 minutes *OR* mix with paddle attachment on Low/Stir 3 minutes, then switch to dough hook and knead 7 minutes on Low/Medium.

•While dough is kneading (or before if kneading by hand) put a couple inches of hot tap water into pressure cooker pan. When dough is done kneading, discard water but do not dry pan. Put dough into a lightly greased bowl, turn to coat, put into pressure cooker pan, set lid on top and let rise 1 hour or until double in size.

•Punch down and pat or roll into a rectangle ½" thick, almost the width of your bread pan. Spread with softened butter to within ½" of edges. Combine nuts, brown sugar and cinnamon and sprinkle evenly over top of buttered dough and pat down. Roll into a loaf, pinch ends and bottom seam to seal and place, seam-side down, into a lightly greased bread pan.

•Put 1 ½ cups water into pressure cooker pan, set in a 1"—2" trivet, lay sling across bottom and up sides for easy access, set bread pan in middle, place lid on top and let rise 45 minutes or until double in size.

•If desired, lay a circle of foil, spritzed with cooking spray on the underside, on top of bread pan but do not attach in any way. Secure lid —MAKE SURE VALVE IS ON SEAL—and cook on High pressure 50 (34) minutes. Quick-release pressure and insert a quick-read thermometer a couple places near center. If below 190°, secure lid, CLOSE VALVE and cook another 5 minutes. Remove to rack, let rest 10 minutes, then remove bread from pan to cool on rack. Drizzle the melted butter and brown sugar in bottom of pan over top of loaf.

VERY CHERRY BUBBLE BREAD

Nutrition Data: Ten Generous Servings; Made with whole milk.
Each: 281 Calories; 7g Protein; 278mg Sodium; 8g Total Fat; 48gCarbs; 1g Fiber

NOTES:_____
_____
_____
_____
_____
_____
_____

VERY CHERRY BUBBLE BREAD

Delicious with whipped cream.
(mini pot measure)

¾ **Cup** (¼ Cup + 1 TBS) **Milk**

¼ (⅛) **Cup Water**

1 (1) **Egg, large**

2 (1) **TBS Butter, softened**

3 (1 ½) **Cups Bread Flour**

2 (1) **TBS Granulated Sugar**

1 (½) **tsp Diastatic Malt Powder**

1 (½) **tsp Salt**

1 *Pkt (1 tsp) **Active Dry Yeast**
   *Pkt. = 2 ¼ tsp

1 21 oz. (½) **Can Cherry Pie Filling**

¼ (⅛) **Cup Granulated Sugar**

1 (½) **tsp Cinnamon**

¼ (⅛) **Cup Sugar**

1 (½) **tsp Cinnamon**

•Put first 9 ingredients in order given in mixer bowl. Mix and knead by hand 10 minutes *OR* mix with paddle attachment 3 minutes on Low/Stir, then switch to dough hook and knead 7 minutes on Low/Medium.

•While dough is kneading, or before if mixing by hand, put a couple inches of hot tap water in cooker pan. When dough is done kneading, discard water but do not dry pan. Put dough ball into a lightly greased bowl, turn to coat, set into cooker pan, place lid on top and let rise 1 hour, or until double in size.

•Generously butter a 6-cup flute pan (mini flute pan). Combine cherry pie filling, sugar and cinnamon in a small bowl. Remove 1 (½) cup and distribute on bottom of flute pan. Set aside the rest.

•While dough is rising, put sugar and cinnamon in a small zip bag and shake to combine. •Punch down dough, pull off small pieces and roll into walnut-size balls. Put them into the sugar bag and when you have 8-10, shake to lightly coat. Distribute balls evenly on top of cherry mixture in flute pan. Continue process until half the dough is gone. Spoon ½ the set-aside cherry mixture into the crevices. Repeat process of rolling and sugar-coating balls until dough is gone, then finish by filling gaps with remaining cherry mixture.

•Put 1 ½ cups water in cooker pan and set in a low trivet (no more than 1" high). Instead of laying the sling across the trivet as usual, lay the sling on the counter and set the fluted pan in the middle. (Another reason why a 2" wide sling is important!) Bring up the sides of the sling and hold tightly against the pan. Lift and set pan into the pressure cooker. Tuck tops of sling to the side for easy access. Place lid on top and let dough rise 45 minutes or until double in size.

•Secure lid —MAKE SURE VALVE IS ON SEAL—and cook on High pressure 35 (24) minutes, then quick-release the pressure. Your creation will be mammoth. Insert quick-read temperature probe two or three places near center. If below 190°, secure lid, CLOSE VALVE and cook another 5 minutes. Carefully grasp the ends of the sling and lift pan out to the counter. Let rest 10 minutes, then place a large plate over the top and invert pan so the cherries are now on top. Let it rest a couple more minutes so cherry sauce can drip onto bread before lifting off the pan. This is a creation to be proud of!

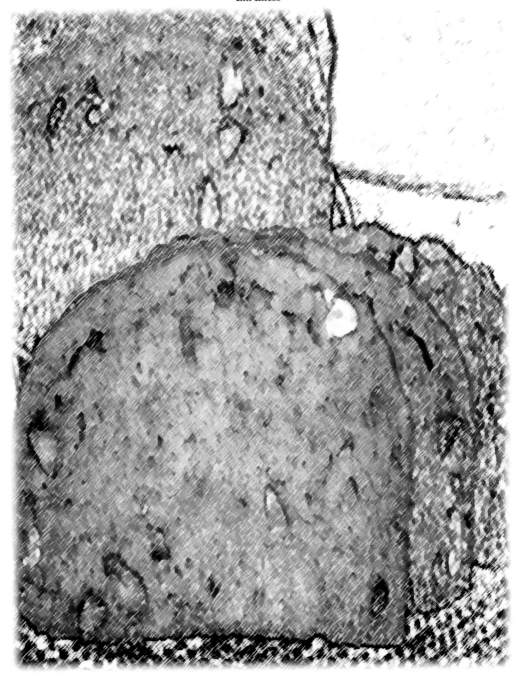

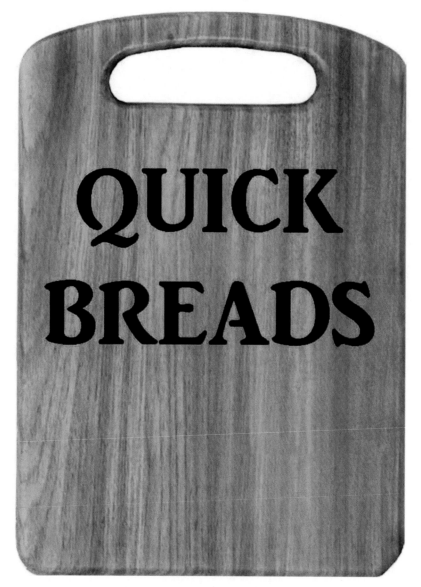

QUICK BREADS

Quick Bread Tip: The texture of the bread beneath the crust is called the crumb. Open crumb is chewier and "holey," like sourdough and French bread. Quick breads should be closed crumb, with a tender, delicate texture. If there are tunnels and holes, the dough has been overmixed, trapping air bubbles that will make the finished bread more tough. Mix just until the flour disappears.

PRUNE NUT BREAD

Nutrition Data: Ten Generous Servings; Made with pecans and coconut oil.
Each: 291 Calories; 4g Protein; 320mg Sodium; 11g Total Fat; 45gCarbs; 2g Fiber

NOTES:_____

_____

_____

_____

_____

_____

_____

PRUNE NUT BREAD

Absolutely fabulous, delectable bread. (mini pot measurement)

¾ Cup (6 TBS) Pecans or Walnuts, chopped

1 (½) Cup Prunes, chopped

¾ Cup (¼ + 2 TBS) Boiling Water

1 1/2 (¾) Cups All Purpose Flour

1 1/2 (¾) tsp Baking Powder

1/2 (¼) tsp Baking Soda

1/2 (¼) tsp Salt

3 (1½) TBS Coconut Oil or Shortening

1 (½) Cup Brown Sugar

2 (1) Eggs, large

1 (½) tsp Vanilla

●In a small bowl, pour boiling water over prunes (I snip with scissors) and set aside.

●In separate bowl put flour, baking powder, baking soda and salt. Mix with fork until well blended. Set aside.

●In mixer bowl put coconut oil/shortening and brown sugar and mix on Medium about 1 minute. Add eggs and vanilla, slowly increase speed to Medium and mix a minute or so until well combined. Add nuts and prunes and mix on Medium another minute, until well combined.

●Remove mixer bowl from stand, add flour mixture and stir until flour is just moistened (can't see it anymore). Do not overmix. Scrape batter into lightly greased bread pan.

●Put 1½ cups water in pressure cooker pan, set in a 1"-2" inch trivet, lay sling across middle and up sides for easy access and set in bread pan.

●If desired lay a circle of foil, spritzed with cooking spray on the underside, on top of bread pan. Do not attach in any way.

●Secure lid—MAKE SURE VALVE IS ON SEAL—and cook on High pressure 60 (40) minutes. Quick-release pressure and insert knife a couple places near center of bread. If it comes out clean (no raw dough on blade), remove bread to trivet and let cool 10 minutes before removing from pan. If knife shows raw dough, not just cooked prune, secure lid, CLOSE VALVE, and cook another 5 minutes.

BANANA NUT BREAD

Nutrition Data: 8 Generous Servings; Made with pecans
Each: 312 Calories; 4g Protein; 458mg Sodium; 11g Total Fat; 43g Carbs;1+g Fiber

NOTES:_____

_____

_____

_____

_____

_____

BANANA NUT BREAD

Extra rich with flavor when it's pressure-cooked! (mini-pot measurement)

2-3 (1 to 1½) **Bananas, over-ripe**

1/3 Cup (3 TBS) **Butter, melted**

2 (1) **Eggs, large**

1 (½) **tsp Vanilla**

½ (¼) **Cup Brown Sugar**

¼ Cup (2 TBS) **Granulated Sugar**

1 ½ (¾) **Cups All-Purpose Flour**

½ (¼) **tsp Salt**

1 ½ (¾) **tsp Baking Soda**

½ (¼) **tsp Baking Powder**

½ (¼) **Cup Chopped Pecans or Walnuts, optional**

●Mash over-ripe bananas with large fork in mixing bowl until smooth. Add melted butter and mix well. Add brown and granulated sugars, eggs and vanilla. Mix until well blended (egg whites are no longer visible in batter).

●In separate bowl put flour, baking soda, baking powder, salt and chopped nuts. Mix well. Add to banana mixture and stir until just moistened (flour no longer visible). DO NOT OVER-MIX.

●Spoon into greased bread pan. Put 1 ½ Cups hot water into pressure pan, set in a 1" to 2" trivet, lay sling across center and up sides for easy access and set bread pan on top.

●If desired lay a circle of foil, spritzed with cooking spray on the underside, on top of bread pan. Do not attach in any way. Secure lid—MAKE SURE VALVE IS ON SEAL—and cook on High pressure 60 (40) minutes. Quick-release pressure and insert knife two places near center. If knife does not withdraw clean (there is uncooked batter on knife), secure lid, CLOSE VALVE and cook another 5 minutes. Lift out to cooling rack, let rest 10 minutes, then remove bread from pan to cool on rack.

MEXICAN FRUIT CAKE

Nutrition Data: Ten Servings
Each: 179 Calories; 2g Protein; 243mg Sodium; 5g Total Fat; 21gCarbs; 1g Fiber

NOTES:_____

_____

_____

_____

_____

_____

_____

MEXICAN FRUIT CAKE with Cream Cheese Frosting

Fast, Easy, Delicious, Decadent This is one of those recipes that people either really love it, or really don't. Obviously I'm in the "love" camp. (mini pot measurement)

1/2 (¼) Can Crushed Pineapple

   (slightly rounded 1 (½) cup)

1 (1) Egg, large

1 (½) Cup Sugar

1/2 (¼) Cup Whole Wheat Flour

1/2 (¼) Cup All Purpose Flour

1/2 (¼) Cup Chopped Nuts

1 (½) tsp Baking Soda

½ (¼) tsp Salt

●Put all ingredients in bowl and combine with a large spoon. Do not overmix. Scoop batter into lightly greased round pan.

●Put 1 ½ cups water in pressure cooker pan and set in a 1" to 2" trivet. Lay sling across middle and up sides for easy access and set cake pan in middle.

●If desired, lay a circle of foil, spritzed with cooking spray on the underside, on top of bread pan. Do not attach in any way. Secure lid —MAKE SURE VALVE IS ON SEAL—and cook on High pressure 55 (37) minutes.

●Quick-release pressure and insert knife a couple places near center. If knife does not come out clean (there is raw dough on blade), secure lid, CLOSE VALVE, and cook another 5 minutes. Lift out to rack, let rest 10 minutes, then remove cake from pan to finish cooling on rack before frosting.

CREAM CHEESE FROSTING

2 oz. (4 TBS) cream cheese (2 TBS)

1/4 Cup (2 TBS) Butter

1 (½) Cup Powdered Sugar

●Mix room-temperature ingredients together until smooth.

CRANBERRY ORANGE BREAD

Nutrition Data: Ten Slices; Made with whole milk
Each: 259 Calories; 4g Protein; 386mg Sodium; 15g Total Fat; 42gCarbs;3g Fiber

NOTES:_____

_____

_____

_____

_____

_____

_____

CRANBERRY ORANGE BREAD

How do I love thee? I can't count all the ways! Makes a beautiful gift. (mini pot measurement)

3/4 Cup (5 TBS) Milk

1/4 Cup (2 TBS) Oil

1 (1) Egg, large

1 (½) Cup Sugar

1 (½) Orange, peeled

1 (½) Cup All Purpose Flour

1 (½) Cup Whole Wheat Flour

1 ½ (¾) tsp Baking Powder

1/2 (¼) tsp Baking Soda

1 (½) tsp Salt

1 (½) Cup Cranberries, fresh or thawed whole

½ (¼) Cup Pecans or Walnuts, chopped

•Break apart a peeled orange (use a citrus zester for decorative accents before peeling, if desired) and put into a food processor. Add oil, milk, sugar and egg. Process 1 minute or until well combined and orange seeds almost disappear. Pour into a bowl and stir in cranberries and nuts.

•In separate bowl put the two flours, baking powder, baking soda and salt. Combine with a fork.

•Stir flour mixture into orange liquids until flour is just moistened and you can no longer see it. Be careful not to overmix.

•Scrape batter into a lightly greased bread pan, sprinkle on orange peel zests if desired. Put 1½ cups water in pressure cooker pan set in a 1" trivet, place sling across center and up sides for easy access and set in bread pan.

•If desired, lay a circle of foil, spritzed on the underside with cooking spray, on top of bread pan. Do not attach in any way; just set it lightly on top. Secure lid—MAKE SURE VALVE IS ON SEAL—and cook on High pressure-60 (40) minutes. Quick-release pressure and insert a knife two or three places near center. If blade does not come out clean (there is uncooked dough on blade), secure lid, CLOSE VALVE, and cook another 5 minutes Remove pan to rack, let cool 10 or so minutes, then remove bread from pan and let cool on rack.

GOLDEN SPOON BREAD

Nutrition Data: Eight Generous Servings; Made with whole milk.
Each: 178 Calories; 6g Protein; 610mg Sodium; 16g Total Fat; 18gCarbs; 1g Fiber

NOTES:_____

_____

_____

_____

_____

_____

_____

GOLDEN SPOON BREAD

Sponge-like, melt-in-your-mouth richness. (mini pot measurement)

¾ (1/3) **Cup Sharp Cheddar Cheese, shredded**

1 (½) **Cup Milk**

2 (1) **TBS Butter**

2 (1) **Eggs, large**

1 TBS (1 1/2 tsp) **Yellow Mustard**

1/2 (¼) **Cup Corn Meal**

¾ **Cup** (6 TBS) **All Purpose Flour**

1 TBS (1 1/2 tsp) **Sugar**

1 (1/2) **tsp Salt**

1 ½ (¾) **tsp Baking Powder**

½ (¼) **tsp Baking Soda**

•Microwave milk and butter until milk is warm enough to melt butter when stirred. Don't scald; we just want nice warm milk.

•Put eggs in mixing bowl and mix vigorously with a fork 1 minute. Add mustard and cheese and stir to combine. Add warm milk/butter and stir until combined.

•In separate bowl put corn meal, flour and all other dry remaining ingredients. Mix with fork until well combined.

•Add flour mixture to egg mixture and fold in with large spoon until flour disappears. *It is important not to overmix*! It will be lumpy. That's good. Scrape batter into a lightly greased stack pan or cake pan.

•Put 1½ cups water in pressure cooker pan, set in a 1" to 2" trivet, place sling across bottom and up sides for easy access. Set in bread pan. If desired, lay a circle of foil, spritzed with cooking spray on the underside, on top of bread pan. Do not attach in any way. Secure lid—MAKE SURE VALVE IS ON SEAL—and cook on High pressure 50 (34) minutes. Quick-release pressure and insert knife a couple places near center. If blade does not come out clean (raw dough is obvious on the blade), secure lid, CLOSE VALVE, and cook another 5 minutes. Lift pan out to rack, let rest 10 minutes, then remove bread from pan to finish cooling on rack (but you don't have to wait; if company's not coming, enjoy a warm slice. slathered with butter. It is SO delectable!)

PUMPKIN PIE BREAD

Nutrition Data: Eight Generous Servings
Each: 229 Calories; 3g Protein; 357mg Sodium; 3g Total Fat; 25gCarbs;   1g Fiber

NOTES:_____

_____

_____

_____

_____

_____

_____

PUMPKIN PIE BREAD

This buoyant pumpkin and spice bread will surprise you with its tender, rich flavor. Top with a large dollop of whipped cream. *It is best cooked in a cake pan or fluted pan.*
(mini pot measurement)

1 (½) **Cup Pumpkin Puree**

1/2 (¼) **Cup Cooking Oil**

1 1/3 (2/3) **Cup Sugar**

2 (1) **Eggs, large**

1 ½ **Cup + 2 TBS All Purpose Flour** (¾ cup + 1 TBS)

1 ½ (¾) **tsp Baking Powder**

¼ (⅛) **tsp Baking Soda**

1 (½) **tsp Salt**

1 (½) **tsp Cinnamon**

1 (½) **tsp Nutmeg**

½ (¼) **tsp Ground Cloves**

¼ (⅛) **tsp Ground Ginger**

•Put egg/s in mixing bowl and whisk vigorously with a fork for 1 minute. Add pumpkin, oil and sugar. Mix with large fork until well blended.

•In separate bowl put flour and all other dry ingredients. Mix thoroughly.

•Add dry ingredients to pumpkin mixture and fold in with a large spoon until flour disappears. *Be careful not to overmix.* Scrape batter into lightly greased pan.

•Put 1 ½ cups water in pressure cooker pan, set in a 1" trivet, lay sling across middle and up sides for easy access and set in bread pan. If desired, place a circle of foil, spritzed with cooking spray on the underside, on top of bread pan. Do not attach in any way.

•Secure lid—MAKE SURE VALVE IS ON SEAL—and cook on High pressure 60 (40) minutes. Quick-release pressure and insert knife a couple places near center. If knife does not come out clean (there is uncooked dough on the blade), secure lid, CLOSE VALVE, and cook another five minutes. Lift bread out to rack, let rest 10 minutes, then remove bread from pan to finish cooling on rack.

GINGERBREAD LOAF WITH LEMON SAUCE

Nutrition Data: Ten Bread Servings; Made with whole milk.
Each: 137 Calories; 3g Protein; 415mg Sodium; 10g Total Fat; 23gCarbs;0g Fiber
LEMON SAUCE: Ten Servings
Each: 60 Calories; 0g Protein; 18mg Sodium; 2g Total Fat; 6g Carbs; 0 g Fiber

NOTES:_____

_____

_____

_____

_____

_____

_____

GINGERBREAD LOAF W/ LEMON SAUCE

Offering two versions of this flavor-rich loaf with only two slight modifications, both forming a wonderful molasses glaze. For regular recipe follow all bold black ingredients. For a denser, more bread-like loaf, substitute the two *measurements in blue. (mini pot measurement)*

1 (½) Cup Milk (2/3 Cup)

2 TBS (1 TBS) Butter

1 (1) Egg, large

¼ Cup (2 TBS) Molasses

1 (2 tsp) TBS Brown Sugar

1 1/2 (¾ Cup) Cups Flour (2 Cups)

1 tsp Salt (½ tsp)

1 tsp Cinnamon (½ tsp)

1 tsp Ground Ginger (½ tsp)

1 ½ tsp Baking Powder (¾ tsp)

½ tsp Baking Soda (¼ tsp)

•Put milk and butter in microwave and heat just until butter melts. Do not scald; we just want very warm milk.

•Put egg in mixing bowl and whisk 1 minute with a fork. Add molasses and brown sugar and mix until combined. Pour in warm milk and butter and mix until blended. Take a moment to breathe in the wonderful aromas.

•In separate bowl put flour and all other dry ingredients. Mix thoroughly with a fork. Add all at once to liquids and mix with a large spoon just until flour disappears. Dense loaf batter will be very thick. *Be careful not to overmix.* Pour or scrape batter into lightly greased bread pan.

•Put 1 ½ cups water into pressure cooker pan, set in a 1" to 2" trivet, lay sling across bottom and up sides for easy access and set bread pan in center. If desired, lay a circle of foil. Spritzed with cooking spray on the underside, on top of bread pan. Do not attach in any way. Secure lid—MAKE SURE VALVE IS ON SEAL—and cook on High pressure 45 (30) minutes. Quick-release pressure and insert knife a couple places near center. If knife does not come out clean (raw dough is evident on the blade), secure lid, CLOSE VALVE, and cook another 5 minutes. Lift out to rack, let rest 10 minutes, then remove bread from pan and let cool on rack. *Option: Serve with Lemon Sauce*

Optional LEMON SAUCE

½ (¼) Cup Sugar — 1 (½) TBS Cornstarch —¼ tsp (pinch) Salt — 1 (½) Cup Boiling Water — 1 ½ TBS (2+ tsp) Lemon Juice — 2 (1) TBS Butter — 1 (½) tsp Lemon Peel/Zest (optional)

•Put sugar, salt and cornstarch in a small pan. Stir to combine. Slowly add boiling water and stir on medium heat until mixture comes to a boil, thickens and turns translucent. Remove from heat, add butter, juice and optional peel. Combine. Serve warm.

APPLE BREAD
Nutrition Data: Eight Generous Servings; Made with whole milk.
Each: 268 Calories; 5g Protein; 626mg Sodium; 11g Total Fat; 46g Carbs; 1g Fiber

NOTES:_____

_____

_____

_____

_____

APPLE BREAD

Company-worthy. One of my favorite comfort foods, usually made in a round stack pan. (mini pot measurement)

2 (1) Cups All Purpose Flour

2 (1) TBS Granulated Sugar

1 ½ (¾) tsp Baking Powder

1 (½) tsp Baking Soda

1 (½) tsp Salt

2 (1) TBS Butter

1 (1) Egg, large

3/4 Cup (5 TBS) Milk

1 TBS (1 ½ tsp) Lemon Juice

***½ (¼) Cup Cinnamon Applesauce**

(*=1 snack cup)

2 (1) Cups Chopped Unpeeled Apple

(about 1 large (small) apple)

½ (¼) Cup Brown Sugar

1 ½ (¾) tsp Cinnamon

½ (¼) tsp Nutmeg

½ (¼) Cup Shredded Cheddar Cheese

•Core apple, chop into small pieces and put into a small bowl. Add brown sugar, cinnamon and nutmeg and stir until apples are coated. Set aside.

•Put milk and butter in microwaveable dish and heat 1 ½ minutes, until butter starts to melt. Stir until butter is melted, then add lemon juice. Stir and set aside.

•In mixing bowl put flour, baking powder, soda and salt. Stir until well combined.

•Put egg in a small bowl and whip with a fork to break up. Add applesauce and sugar and whisk until combined. Add milk mixture and stir until combined.

•Pour liquids over flour mixture and stir with a large spoon until flour disappears. *Do not overmix.* Batter will be very thick and sticky.

•With a large spoon spread half of batter in a lightly-greased round pan to edges of pan. Distribute half the apples over the top, then half the shredded cheese. Using two spoons, drop dollops of batter over the top, around and around until evenly distributed. Scatter remaining apples over the top, then drizzle on the sugared juice in bottom of bowl. Sprinkle top with remaining cheese.

•Put 1½ cups water in pressure cooker pan, set in a 1" to 2" trivet, place sling across bottom and up sides for easy access and set bread pan in center. If desired, lay a circle of foil, spritzed with cooking oil on the underside, on top of bread pan. Do not attach in any way. Secure lid—MAKE SURE VALVE IS ON SEAL—and cook on High pressure 60 (40) minutes. Remove to rack, let rest 10 minutes, then remove bread from pan to cool on rack. Serve warm.

CARROT RAISIN BREAD

Nutrition Data: 8 Generous Servings; Made with whole milk.
Each: 274 Calories; 4g Protein; 537mg Sodium; 11g Total Fat; 54g Carbs;1+g Fiber

NOTES:_____

_____

_____

_____

_____

_____

_____

CARROT RAISIN BREAD

Melt-in-your-mouth delicious. Slather with cream cheese and enjoy warm. Beautiful cooked in a fluted pan. (mini-pot measurement)

1 2/3 Cups (1/2 Cup + 1/3 Cup) **All Purpose Flour**

1 ½ (¾) **tsp Baking Powder**

½ (¼) **tsp Baking Soda**

1 (½) **tsp Salt**

1 (½) **tsp Cinnamon**

1 (½) **tsp Pumpkin Pie Spice**

1 (½) **Cup Raisins**

½ Cup (3 TBS) **Milk**

¼ Cup (2 TBS) **Butter**

1 (1) **Egg, large**

¾ Cup (6 TBS) **Granulated Sugar**

¾ (not quite 1/2) **Cup Carrots, finely chopped**

●Put milk and butter in a small microwave-safe bowl and heat 1 minute, until butter starts to melt. Remove and stir until butter is melted.

●In separate bowl put flour, baking powder and soda, salt and spices. Stir until well blended and set aside.

●Put egg in a mixing bowl and whip with fork until broken down. Add sugar and stir well to combine. Add milk/butter, carrots and raisins and stir until well mixed.

●Add flour mixture to liquids all at once and stir with a large spoon just until flour disappears. *Do not overmix.* Scrape batter into a greased 6-cup fluted pan (or mini pan of your choice).

●Put 1½ cups water in pressure cooker pan and set in a 1" trivet. The fluted pan is difficult to place into the cooker with your hands, so lay sling on the counter, place pan in center and draw up sling tightly against sides of pan. Lift and lower pan down into cooker pan. Fold back sling for easy access. If desired, lay a circle of foil, spritzed with cooking spray on the underside, on top of bread pan. Do not attach in any way.

●Secure lid—MAKE SURE VALVE IS ON SEAL—and cook on High pressure 45 (30) minutes. Quick-release pressure and insert an instant-read thermometer a couple places near center. If knife does not come out clean (there is raw dough on the blade), secure lid, CLOSE VALVE and cook another 5 minutes. Lift out to rack, let rest 10 minutes, then remove bread from pan to rack. Slice and enjoy when warm enough to handle.

BANANA BRAN BREAD

Nutrition Data: Eight Generous Servings; Made with whole milk.
Each: 327 Calories; 5g Protein; 346mg Sodium; 14g Total Fat; 55g Carbs;2.5g Fiber

NOTES:_____

_____

_____

_____

_____

_____

_____

BANANA BRAN BREAD

Chewy, moist, great anytime. (mini pot measurement)

1 ¾ Cups (¾ Cup + 2 TBS) **All Purpose Flour**

¾ Cup (6 TBS) **Granulated Sugar**

2 ½ (1 ¼) **tsp Baking Powder**

½ (¼) **tsp Baking Soda**

½ (¼) **tsp Salt**

1 ½ (¾ Cup) **Cups Bran Flakes**

⅓ (¼) **Cup Walnuts or Pecans**

½ Cup Milk (3 TBS)

1 (1) **Egg, large**

¼ Cup (2 TBS) **Butter**

1 (½) **tsp Vanilla**

2 (1) **Bananas, overripe**

•Put milk and butter in microwave-safe dish and heat 1 minute, until butter starts to melt. Remove and stir until butter melts. Set aside.

•In small mixing bowl combine flour, baking powder, soda and salt. Stir until well mixed.

•Put bananas in larger mixing bowl and smash until mushy. Stir in egg, sugar and vanilla until egg disappears. Add bran flakes and nuts. Pour milk mixture over top and stir until well combined.

•Add flour mixture all at once and stir just until flour disappears. *Do not overmix.* Scrape batter into a buttered or lightly greased bread pan (I use a 6-cup fluted pan).

•Put 1 ½ cups water in pressure cooker pan and set in a 1" to 2" trivet. Lay sling across bottom and up sides for easy access, *OR*, if using a fluted pan, lay sling on counter, put pan in middle, hold sling tightly against pan, lift and lower into cooker pan. If desired, lay a circle of foil, spritzed with cooking spray on the underside, on top of bread pan. Do not attach in any way.

•Secure lid —MAKE SURE VALVE IS ON SEAL—and cook on High pressure 50 (34) minutes. Quick-release pressure and insert a knife two or three places near center. (If knife does not come out clean (there is raw dough on the blade), secure lid, CLOSE VALVE and cook another 5 minutes. Lift out bread to rack, let cool 10 minutes, then remove bread from pan and let cool to cutting temperature (how long you are willing to wait).

CORN BREAD/COUNTRY STYLE

Nutrition Data: Eight Generous Servings; Made with whole milk and coconut oil.
Each: 165 Calories; 4g Protein; 513mg Sodium; 11g Total Fat; 25gCarbs;1g Fiber

NOTES:_____

_____

_____

_____

_____

_____

_____

CORN BREAD, COUNTRY STYLE

For a real down-home taste treat, grease pan with bacon drippings and/or substitute bacon drippings for coconut oil/shortening. *(mini pot measure)*

1 (½) Cup All Purpose Flour

¾Cup (6 TBS) Corn Meal

2 (1) TBS Granulated Sugar

1 (½) tsp Salt

1 TBS (1 ½ tsp) Baking Powder

1 (½) Cup Milk

1 (1) Egg

2 (1) TBS Coconut Oil or Shortening

•Put flour, corn meal, salt and baking powder in a small mixing bowl. Mix until well-blended. Set aside.

•Put milk and coconut oil or shortening in a microwave-safe dish and heat a minute or so, until oil starts to melt. Remove and stir until completely melted. Set aside.

•Put egg in a mixing bowl and whisk until well beaten. Add sugar and combine. Add milk mixture and mix until combined.

•Add flour mixture all at once and stir just until flour disappears. *Do not overmix.* Scrape batter into a lightly greased pan.

•Put 1 ½ cups water in pressure cooker pan, lay sling across bottom and up sides for easy access and set bread pan in middle. If desired, lay a circle of foil, spritzed with cooking spray on the underside, on top of bread pan. Do not attach in any way. Secure lid —MAKE SURE VALVE IS ON SEAL—and cook on High pressure 25 (17) minutes. Quick-release pressure and insert a knife 2 or 3 places near center. If knife does not come out clean (there is raw dough on the blade), secure lid, CLOSE VALVE and cook another 5 minutes. Remove to rack, let rest 10 minutes, then remove bread from pan.

CORN BREAD, CAKE–LIKE

Nutrition Data: Eight Generous Servings; Made with whole milk and coconut oil. Each: 331 Calories; 5g Protein; 566mg Sodium; 22g Total Fat; 45gCarbs;1g Fiber

NOTES:_____

_____

_____

_____

_____

_____

_____

CORN BREAD, CAKE-LIKE

Says it. (mini pot measurement)

½ Cup (¼) Cornmeal

1 ½ Cups (¾) All Purpose Flour

1 TBS (1 ½ tsp) Baking Powder

1 tsp (½) Salt

1 Cup (½) Milk

¼ Cup (2 TBS) Butter

¼ Cup (2TBS) Coconut or Vegetable Oil

2 (1) Eggs, large

¾ Cup (6 TBS) Granulated Sugar

1 (½) TBS Honey

•Put milk and butter *(and coconut oil if using instead of vegetable oil)* in a microwave-safe dish and heat 1 ½ minutes, until butter starts to melt. Remove, stir until butter melts and set aside.

•In small mixing bowl put cornmeal, flour, salt and baking powder. Stir with fork until well blended. Set aside.

•Put eggs in a regular mixing bowl and whisk until well broken down. Add honey and sugar *(and vegetable oil if coconut oil not added to milk)* and whisk until combined. Add milk mixture and whisk until well combined.

•Add flour mixture all at once and stir with large spoon just until flour disappears. *Do not overmix.* Batter will be lumpy. Scrape into a lightly-greased bread pan (I use a 7 ½" stack pan in a 6 qt cooker, a small fluted in a mini pot).

•Put 1 ½ cups water in pressure cooker pan, set in a 1" to 2" trivet, lay sling across bottom and up sides for easy access and set bread pan in center. If desired lay a circle of foil, spritzed with cooking spray on the underside, on top of bread pan. Do not attach in any way.

•Secure lid—MAKE SURE VALVE IS ON SEAL—and cook on high pressure 35 (24) minutes. Quick-release pressure and insert a knife near center. If knife does not come out clean (there is raw batter on blade), secure lid, CLOSE VALVE and cook another 5 minutes. Lift out to rack, let cool 10 minutes, then remove bread from pan to continue cooling on rack.

IRISH SODA BREAD

Nutrition Data: Eight Generous Servings
Each: 210 Calories; 4g Protein; 382mg Sodium; 4g Total Fat; 38gCarbs; 1g Fiber

NOTES:_____

_____

_____

_____

_____

_____

_____

IRISH SODA BREAD

I have to admit that I never baked or tasted Irish Soda Bread until developing recipes for this cookbook. The sound never appealed to me, but because it is so popular I wanted to include it. I certainly did not expect to love it as much as I do now. The combination of flavors hits all the right taste-buds. It's wonderful plain. It's crunchy-wonderful toasted. I hope you enjoy it as well! (mini pot measure)

2 ¼ (1 ⅛) **Cups All Purpose Flour**

1 ½ tsp (¾ tsp) **Baking Powder**

½ (¼) **tsp Baking Soda**

½ (¼) **tsp Salt**

1 TBS (2 tsp) **Caraway Seeds**

1 (1) **Egg, large**

¼ Cup (2 TBS) **Sugar**

1 (½) **Cup Buttermilk**

2 (1) **TBS Butter**

½ (¼) **Cup Raisins**

•Put buttermilk and butter in a microwave-safe dish and heat for 1 minute, until butter starts to melt. Remove and stir until butter is melted. Stir in raisins and set aside.

•In a small mixing bowl combine flour, baking powder and soda, salt and caraway seeds with a fork until well blended. Set aside.

•In a larger mixing bowl whisk egg and sugar together until well blended. Add buttermilk/raisins and stir in thoroughly. Add flour mixture all at once and stir with a large spoon until flour is just moistened. *Do not overmix.* Scrape batter into a lightly greased pan (I use a stack pan).

•Put 1 ½ cups water in pressure cooker pan, set in a 1" to 2" high trivet, lay sling across bottom and up sides for easy access and set bread pan in center. If desired, lay a circle of foil, spritzed with cooking spray on the underside, on top to bread pan. Do not attach in any way.

•Secure lid—MAKE SURE VALVE IS ON SEAL—and cook on High pressure 50 (34) minutes. Quick release pressure and insert a knife one or two places near center. If knife does not come out clean (there is raw batter on blade), secure lid, CLOSE VALVE and cook another 5 minutes. Lift out to cooling rack, let rest 10 minutes, then remove bread from pan to finish cooling on rack.

CHOCOLATE ZUCCHINI BREAD

Nutrition Data: Eight Generous Servings
Each: 280 Calories; 3g Protein; 563mg Sodium; 12g Total Fat; 41gCarbs;1g Fiber

NOTES:_____
_____
_____
_____
_____
_____

CHOCOLATE ZUCCHINI BREAD

Rich, tender and moist. More brownie than bread. Yum! (mini pot measure)

1 (½) Cup Sugar

1/2 (¼) Cup Butter

1 (1) Egg, large

1 (½) tsp Vanilla

1 ¼ Cups (½ Cup + 2 TBS) Flour

¼ Cup (2 TBS) Cocoa

1 (½) tsp Salt

1 ½ tsp (¾ tsp) Baking Powder

½ tsp (¼ tsp) Baking Soda

1 (½) tsp Cinnamon

*1 (½) Cup Zucchini, shredded

(*if using frozen, thaw, put into a strainer and press out excess liquid)

●Melt butter in a microwave-safe dish (30-60 seconds) and set aside.

●Put flour, baking powder and soda, cinnamon, salt and cocoa in a small bowl and stir thoroughly with a fork to combine.

●Put egg and sugar in larger mixing bowl and whisk until combined. Mix in vanilla and melted butter and stir to combine. Stir in zucchini.

●Add flour mixture all at once and stir with a large spoon just until flour disappears. Do not overmix. Batter will be thick. Scrape into a lightly greased pan.

●Put 1 ½ cups water in cooker pan. Set in a 1" to 2" trivet. Lay sling across bottom and up sides for easy access. Set bread pan in center. If desired lay a circle of foil, spritzed with cooking spray on the underside, on top of bread pan. Do not attach in any way.

●Secure lid—MAKE SURE VALVE IS ON SEAL—and cook on High pressure 60 (40) minutes. Quick-release pressure and insert a knife 2 or 3 places near center. If knife does not come out clean (there is uncooked batter on blade), secure lid, CLOSE VALVE and cook another 5 minutes. Lift bread pan out to rack, let rest 10 minutes, then remove bread from pan and let cool completely before slicing.

EM ELLESS BIOGRAPHY

In her first three cookbooks, Author Em Elless specialized in low-carb gluten-free recipes, a term long considered an oxymoron until the publication of her first book, "Muffins to Slim By." In her newest breakthrough collection, Elless takes a giant step away from special-diet recipes to introduce yet another first-of-its-kind, "The Pressure Cooker Yeast and Quick Bread Cookbook," an illustrated how-to of classic favorites.

With no formal training, Elless spent decades teaching herself culinary techniques many considered impossible to achieve, discovering by trial and error the methods that do not work, and why, and the joy of cooking when they do. "Instant Pots have opened new doors to endless creative possibilities. This is absolutely the best time to be a cook!"

Over a lifetime of artistic endeavors, from fine art and cartooning (the "Donna Quixote" series in the National Museum of Women in the Arts magazine) to free-lance and humor writing in countless venues, Elless has used variations of her name, Marjorie L. Smith. Her cookbook pen name, Em Elless, is the sound of her initials, MLS, which she tried using but was repeatedly mistaken for the Multiple Listing Service. She is aided in the kitchen by her loyal dog, Gaby, who generously donates her time testing samples.

Index

41715415R00062

Made in the USA
Middletown, DE
08 April 2019